Weenie
FAITH

How God Can Use Wimps to Conquer Giants

Brooke Grangard

Published in association with Pinefarm Publishing.

ISBN 978-0-578-65773-8

INTRODUCTION

In the early winter of 2018, I felt a lump in my left breast. After various tests, it was concluded that the lump was an aggressive form of cancer which had already spread to my lymph nodes. As an ordained minister and former missionary, one would think that upon hearing this horrible news, faith would naturally arise. I wish I could say that was the case, but it was not. Faith did not arise at that moment. In fact, terror did.

Though God had walked me through various hardships in the past, I found that as each new one came, greater amounts of courage were required. And I was fairly certain that I did not have enough to defeat the one on hand.

I began to search through various Christian teachings, watching videos and listening to podcasts about faith. How can we get more of it? What do we do when we doubt? Can we still move mountains if we are found lacking? I listened to so many preachers until I became convinced that my future success or failure all hinged on my ability to produce enough of this mystical substance called faith.

It wasn't until I came back to the Lord with my questions that I realized my breakthrough could never be dependent upon me. I would never measure up. My victory was and always had been dependent upon him. God had already provided everything that I needed to see my request answered, and he would show me how to walk the path laid before me. Once I took my eyes off the waves and off my puny self, I was able to see just how loving and powerful he is.

This book is not a self-help book because I have no idea how to help myself, much less try to help you. This book is also not a collection of all of my heroic moments. Most of the stories that I tell are about me trying to run away from my giants with my tail tucked between my legs. I am not a hero, but I know Someone who is.

This book is my attempt to share my journey with others and show that you do not have to have it all together to see God move your mountains. You just need to stay close enough to him until he brings about his purposes in and through you.

I pray that God will break through in your life the way that he did in mine.

Until All is Made New,
Brooke

Chapter One

DRUMMING UP FAITH

"Faith is taking the first step, even when you don't see the whole staircase."

Martin Luther King, Jr.

The Making of a Weenie

I grew up in Colorado, primarily in Durango, Colorado. Durango is a small mountain town in the southwestern part of Colorado that attracts tourists year round. In the summer, they come to our area for the hiking, the mountain biking, and the white-water rafting. In the winter, they come for the skiing, the ice-climbing, and the hot springs. I would call it the Colorado of Colorado, in the sense that people move from all over the country to Colorado so that they can enjoy the outdoors, and Coloradoans move from all over the state to Durango so that they can enjoy the outdoors. It's another level of outdoorsy-ness. You don't drive to the mountains because you live in the mountains.

By Durango's standards, I am not outdoorsy. However, I have discovered in my many years away from home that anywhere else to which I travel, people consider me to be just that. I hike, ski, enjoy camping. I once took a trap-shooting/fly-fishing class as my PE elective in college. But in Durango, this is all normal. It's as common as having an SUV. To be considered *truly* outdoorsy in Durango, you have to have a car that's worth only a quarter of the value of the gear that is being hauled on top of it. And you must spend all of your spare time doing something outside of the four walls your house- something that is hard and mildly terrifying and makes you sweat (sun-bathing not included.)

As teenagers with a lot of spare time, we rarely went to the movies or roamed around the mall like most young ones around the nation do. Instead, my friends and I would midnight raft over the rapids of our river, jump from 50-foot cliffs into water that was actually just melted snow, and ice climb up 100-foot frozen waterfalls.

One would think with this kind of robust upbringing that I would now possess a hearty courage that was able to withstand whatever life could throw at me. Unfortunately, that was not the case. I discovered early on that I was, in fact, a weenie. I was *never* the one to suggest these activities. I would go along with them because for some reason I continued to call these maniacs my friends. And sure, it was fun at times, when the death-defying activities were over and I was still breathing with all limbs intact, but I never had this inner sense of confidence that allowed these adventures to be truly exciting. Most of the time, I was on the verge of panic.

And I had instituted boundaries for these activities. There were certain limits that I was not willing to push. The main one being any activity that relied on my athletic prowess for a positive outcome. In no way did I trust myself to be able to produce the skills necessary to perform said activity and come out alive.

Sure, I would cliff jump, but if it relied on my ability to launch myself off the edge at just the right angle or be doomed to crash into the craggy boulders below, I was out! If it involved making sure that I sprung out far enough away from the cliff's rim or else I would land in the shallow water instead of the desirable *deep* water that was just beyond, I was done. It's not that I *couldn't* do these things. I was a normal healthy teenager. It's just that I was not going to bet my life on *my own ability* to produce it at just the right moment. I'd rather just climb back down the cliff, like a weenie, life intact.

I've continued to live this way as I've aged. I have no intention of trying to prove myself as brave or adventurous any longer. I don't like to be scared. I am opposed to pain. I don't run marathons because there is too much exhaustion and sweat involved. I've never experienced the mythical second wind that runners speak of when they've pushed past their own limits and their bodies somehow revive themselves. My body always tells me to sit down and shut up!

I don't do blood or wounds. I can barely put a band aid on my own child without gagging. I have no delusion of being the hero. When my (then) 3-year-old son swallowed a LEGO and sought me out for comfort, I began to scream for my husband and search online for every possible horrendous outcome, causing everyone in my family even greater stress and fear. I wonder how the Proverbs 31 woman would have reacted?

5

I like to be prepared. I try to plan everything out so that I am ready for whatever may come at us. Snacks and water bottles, check. Umbrellas and raincoats (even though it's 80 degrees with no hint of rain), check. Snow boots and mittens and a shovel to dig us out in case we run into an avalanche. (I'm honestly not too far from that.)

Yet somehow, despite these wimpy attributes, God has called and used me to accomplish feats that are way beyond my comfort zone: living and working in a closed nation as a missionary for over ten years, training up young people from many nations to follow God, walking through the loss of two babies, grieving the death of my mother whilst I was pregnant with my daughter, and overcoming the hardest fight of my life as I was diagnosed with and treated for a very aggressive form of cancer. How could a weenie not only survive but actually find victory in the midst of so much?

I'll tell you friends, it was not me! As one who has believed in and walked with God for the majority of my life, I often questioned how I could possibly muster up enough faith to get to the promises that seemed to await me on the other side of my pain. When life unraveled, I did not have the power to weave it back together. I was a self-proclaimed weenie.

I turned to other well-known Christian teachers to help me along on my journey. Some of their stories encouraged me, but many only served to plunge me into greater despair. Often the message that came through was either one of self-reliance to change my circumstances or a fatalistic acceptance of them. Neither of these sermons seemed to preach when held up in light of how Jesus taught. Something was off.

Anyone who takes the time to read through the account of Jesus' life as described in the Gospels can clearly see that faith is in fact a big part of obtaining that for which we hope (and we only need a smidge of it), but just as equally true is the certainty that we, in no way, shape, or form, can achieve it on our own. I was unsure at how those two parts fit together to make a whole, and there's nothing like a life-threatening illness with a husband and two small children in tow to thrust one into studying the Bible like it ain't been studied by these hands before!

Somewhere in the mystery of God and mankind, he has designed it so that we have access into this mystical kingdom where good can actually come out of whatever horrible situation that life presents to us. Yet in the same breath, he has also assured us that we can in no way achieve these miracles on our own. Money in a fish's mouth, a mud mask that heals a man's blindness, and stinky corpses coming back from the dead. Way out of our league. But *in* our league, *if we have faith*. What the what? I know. Believe me dear reader, I know.

Make the leap off the cliff, we must. Have our survival reliant only on our own ability to land in the exact spot where the deep water resides, we must not. So how do we live in this dichotomy?

The answer, my friends, is so good. Get ready to lighten your loads as we unpack it throughout the rest of this book. It's one that gives great hope, especially to those who feel they don't make the cut. And to my fellow weenies, get ready to exhale because relief is on the way. Or as God says it in Isaiah 41:14, "So don't be afraid, little worms *(that's what God called us, not me)*, I myself will help you."

Trusting the Faithful One

It's not dependent on us; it's dependent upon his faithfulness. In Second Timothy 2:13, we read, "If we are faithless, he remains faithful, for he cannot deny himself." God is faithful to us because he is faithful. That sounds simple, but that is the source of our greatest hope. He cannot deny himself. His nature is to be faithful. He cannot *not* be faithful. He cannot be *un*faithful. He must remain unwavering and committed because that is who he is, and he does not change. I want to be found loyal to Jesus, but sometimes I doubt how far I am really willing to follow. My confidence resides in the truth that his Spirit lives within me.

We change. We can lose heart. We can become discouraged. On the flip side, we can also grow in faith. We can have increasing revelation of who he is and what he can do. But God cannot grow. He already operates at his maximum capacity. His faithfulness is already on full throttle. It is impossible for him to break a promise. It is impossible for him to change. He has, is, and always will be the same faithful God. Grasping this knowledge with our hearts makes it easier to trust him.

The dictionary defines faith as "confidence or trust in a person or thing." That's what it boils down to. Faith is putting your trust in a person or thing. We have faith in God (meaning that we can *trust* him) because he shows himself faithful to us, globally as mankind and personally in our everyday lives.

Let us consider again the faithfulness of God to us as mankind. I think this area of his faithfulness is often overlooked because it is assumed. Every day the sun rises, and every evening it sets. We do not wonder if it will happen again tomorrow. Every season as the earth rotates around the sun, God proves to us that

He will not let us fall. As the stars appear to plot out the night sky, as the springtime rains come and the wild animals birth their young, as the harvest approaches and we gain food for the winter months, we again rest assured that our God is trustworthy. Psalm 19 actually says that these very heavens are "pouring forth speech" and "making him known," "declaring" or "proclaiming" to the whole world that he is faithful.

Most days, I take these divine attributes for granted. I don't lie in bed at night worrying if our planet will still be circling in its orbit when I wake the next morning. I'm not concerned that gravity will suddenly cease to exist or the magnetic pull of the moon on the oceans' tides will unexpectedly stop. I subconsciously expect God to be faithful throughout the rhythms of life that he has set into motion. It's important for us as humans, every once in a while, to stand in awe of who he is and wonder again at his amazing standard of consistency.

Sometimes when I take a drive through the mountains or head south into the desert area, I look out my window and wonder what God must have seen here hundreds and thousands of years ago. He knew every sparrow that flew in those ancient skies, and he knew every hair on each person's head who walked those ancient paths. And he still does. We must remind our souls again that he is indeed faithful. Even if we have never seen faithfulness modeled by even one person on this earth, we can still know and believe that he will not let us down. His creation proves to us that he is not a flake.

When I get into my car, I have faith that it will get me to where I need to go. When my best friend tells me that she will meet me at our local coffee shop at 10 am, I have faith that she will be there. Why? Because both my car and my best friend have proven to me that they are *faithful*. It would be foolish to put my faith in someone or something that have shown me otherwise. If I find a person to be fickle, I will not trust them. I can love them (bless their hearts), but I don't have to trust them. Trust is built when a person or thing proves to be loyal and able fulfill their promises.

I was fortunate enough to have grown up with a father who kept his promises. I know this is not the case for everyone. I believe this is one of the reasons why it was easy for me, from an early age, to believe that God would do what he said he was going to do. When I went away to college, my parents and I made the agreement that we would split the costs of my tuition. At the beginning of each semester, my dad would put their half of the bill into my bank account. At times, he would tell me which day that he planned to deposit the check.

I trusted that when that date came, the money would be there. I wrote a check to my university in full confidence that the money was in the account. And it was. It always was. My father had proven his trustworthiness to me over a lifetime of keeping his promises. I had no reason to doubt him.

We have absolutely no reason to doubt God, but not all of us know God in this way. I've walked with God for most of my life, but I still see only a glimpse of who he is. If you were not raised with the advantage of having a parent model to you what faithfulness looks like, ask God to fill that gap. Even if we did have faithful family members or authority figures, we can still ask God to show us how trustworthy he is in a new way.

That's On You

"The Lord did not set his affection on you and choose you because you were more numerous than the other peoples, for you were the fewest of all people. But because the Lord loved you and kept the oath He swore to your fathers…"
Deuteronomy 7:7-8a

These verses in Deuteronomy give me great comfort. God did not choose the Israelites because they were something special or possessed some amazing quality. In fact, it was quite the opposite. Israel was the smallest tribe in the area. And if you have even glanced at the book of Exodus, it doesn't take long to see that they spent most of their time whining about and doubting what God would and could do for them. Moses himself doubted God. It's almost as if God chose the weakest bunch of people on the planet just to showcase what he could do.

The Lord rescued them because of *his own* goodness. It was not because of theirs. He had made a promise to the nation of Israel that he was going to love and protect them, and even though they completely broke their side of the bargain time and time again, God continued to remain faithful. This is very comforting news.

Now some may argue that we do have a part to play in this tango of faith, and I would say to them, "Yes, I agree." We do have a part to play. When God parted the Red Sea, the Israelites had to walk through on dry ground. God's part was big, their part was small. God was doing all the heavy lifting. Their responsibility was basically just to take advantage of what God had done for them. He is the rescuer. Or if you are a grammar nerd, he is the verb and we are merely the object of that verb. He is the mighty deliverer. We are the namby-pambies that need delivering. But it's true, we must allow ourselves to be rescued.

I have come to believe that when God was weaving me together in my mother's womb, he looked down the road towards the future of our family and remembered that in a couple of years, he would be stitching together another child. A brother. And this brother would be created with a different genetic make-up than mine. Just enough ingredients to be real siblings on all the DNA tests yet with one very distinct characteristic that would set us apart: this brother would, by nature, not be a weenie.

God must have known what was coming and determined that we would meet the quota of courage that each family is allowed once this son was born, so he graciously saved the heaping tablespoon for my brother and gave just a little pinch to me. That would be enough for what I would be required to do. I assume God figured that he'd just make up for my lack with divine help.

From an early age, it was clear that my brother did not have the normal inhibitions that most children do- the fear factor, if you will. And I'm not even referring to the *bad* kind of fear, the paranoia that can hold us back from all the good that life has to offer. I'm talking about *all fear,* the healthy kind of fear, the fear that says don't jump off a moving train. Or don't climb the top of your grandfather's 90-foot-tall silo when you are only three-years-old. Or don't go bear-hunting with the bow and arrow that you just purchased a month ago and are not adept in using. Or don't run into a burning house. Hmmm, those sound very specific. Ah yes, it's because all of them are stunts that my brother has attempted in the past and the last one he currently does for a living.

He is a lot of the reason that I have any courageous tales under my own personal story-telling belt. There are very few men in my life that I would allow to convince me (or shame me) to take part in ridiculous escapades such as ice climb a 100-foot frozen waterfall, or ski in a blizzard, or agree to be pulled in a trailer that he had hitched up behind his four-wheeler and proceeded to drive 40-mph on the old, pothole infested dirt road near our house. I honestly don't know why I even entertain any of his suggestions! There's something about a brother's influence that can make one agree to plans that, upon commencing, one realizes how foolish these said plans are.

He actually just recently received an award from the fire chief in Austin, Texas, the city where he currently resides, for a courageous water rescue. There was a man stuck in the middle of a raging, flooded river at night. Plan A and plan B had failed, so plan C was to literally tie a rope around my brother's waist, have him swim out into the white water (avoiding the downed barb wire fence as he went) and somehow get this guy back to land. Did I mention that my brother *volunteered* for this? Needless to say, the plan worked (which is why my brother was still around to receive the award). Basically, he now gets paid as an adult for everything he used to get in trouble for as a kid.

What does this have to do with faith? Well, I'm getting to that. I'm going to draw an analogy now between what my brother does and what God does. If you are a citizen of Austin and you find yourself in need of deliverance, whether it be a burning house, a chemical fire in your workplace, or a flooded river, my brother or some other alpha-person in his line of duty will come and rescue you. If you cannot save yourself, if you are doomed without the help of external aid, all you must do is dial 9-1-1 and some strong, capable, and highly-trained human will save you in your hour of need. Your only part to play in the act is to *let yourself be rescued.* If you refuse help, your life may be in jeopardy. We must let ourselves be rescued.

> *"He reached down from on high*
> *and took hold of me;*
> *he drew me out of deep waters.*
> *He rescued me from my powerful enemy,*
> *from my foes, who were too strong for me.*
> *They confronted me in the day of my disaster,*
> *but the Lord was my support.*
> *He brought me out into a spacious place;*
> *he rescued me because he delighted in me."*
> Psalm 18:16-20

I have a confession to make: when authors type out Bible verses in their books, I often just skip over them! Oops! So if you are like me and didn't read the verse that I typed out above, please just keep Psalm 18 in your back pocket for when you need saving. It is such a powerful image of the way that God parts the clouds to rescue us.

God rescues us because he delights in us! We are his children! He doesn't hesitate to go all mama-bear on our enemies. God is not trying to bring us down. He is our biggest fan! Any theology that says otherwise is *wrong*! He is for us and NOT against us. If he gave us his only Son, why would he hold anything else back from us? If he tests us, it's because he knows that we can pass the test! It's not God who is stealing, killing, and destroying; that work is reserved for the Enemy of our souls.

God wants to deliver you from any giant that you are facing. He wants to bring down our Goliaths, but we must let him. That is our part to play. We show up and God does everything else. That is my understanding of faith. If I can just manage to stay in the game, God comes through. And even it's the Holy Spirit helping me; it's not even my own ability. There, that's it. That's the whole message of this book. God is our savior. We just need to let ourselves be saved.

Jesus and the Little Faiths

Jesus was always super kind to the people who needed him. The ones who knew they were sick or broken or sinful. Jesus never turned one of them away. He healed EVERY. SINGLE. ONE.

Shortly after I was diagnosed with breast cancer, I remember listening to a preacher sharing about the importance of faith and how unbelief can keep us from what God has for us. That evening I told my husband, Rich, that I felt I just didn't have enough faith to see Jesus heal me on the spot, even though I so wanted that kind of faith. My wise spouse graciously pointed out the fact that not everyone who came to Jesus for healing had perfect faith and zero doubt, but Jesus still healed them all.

Some of the people that came to Jesus were faith-rockstars! Jesus himself was even amazed by their faith and commended them for it! People like the centurion who had an uncanny understanding of Jesus' authority or the Gentile woman who argued with him about crumbs and dogs, convincing him to heal her child. But other people who came to Jesus were definitely in the weenie category.

Think of the man that asked Jesus to heal his son. In the same breath, he's telling Jesus that he believes, but he needs help with his unbelief (Mark 9:24). Or Mary and Martha who surely saw Jesus perform many miracles, yet did not believe that Jesus could bring their brother back to life. Despite their doubts, Jesus still answered the request that each one brought before him. He did not turn them away merely because they couldn't believe in him perfectly.

Jesus said it would only take a mustard seed of faith to move a mountain. I believe that was meant to be an encouragement. Meaning that you don't even need very much of it to see God come through. That is hopeful!

Even the twelve disciples, who literally walked with the Son of God throughout his entire ministry and saw him perform so many miracles that they can't even be contained in all the books written in all the world (John 21:25) experienced unbelief. In fact, the sixth chapter of Mark seems to draw attention to the fact that merely witnessing miracles is not enough to produce faith.

The disciples had just watched Jesus feed at least 5,000 people with only five loaves of bread and two fish. After the crowd was dismissed, Jesus asked his disciples to get into a boat while he went away by himself to pray for a while. As the night progressed, the waves picked up and the disciples were struggling. Jesus went out to them walking on the water, as you do. The disciples were terrified, thinking he was a ghost until he tells them to not be afraid- it's just him! I like how *The Voice Compass Bible* translation draws out verses 51 and 52 of the chapter:

He walked across the water to the boat; and as soon as He stepped aboard, the contrary wind ceased its blowing. They were greatly astonished; although they had just witnessed the miracle of Jesus feeding 5,000 with bread and fish, and other signs besides, they didn't understand what it all meant and their hearts remained hard.

The commentary for this study Bible goes onto explain it:

Like the Israelites in the Old Testament, the disciples are discovering the truth that miracles don't produce faith. As Jesus so often points out, the process works the other way around: it's faith that produces miracles. Miracles are only signs- evidence of truth that you have to know before the miracle. As long as the disciples are still in doubt about who Jesus is, they find their faith constantly challenged and frequently wavering. It will not be until after the resurrection, the greatest miracle of all, that they will come to recognize and believe in Jesus for who He is; and then their hearts will at last open.

And it's not until they are filled with the Holy Spirit that they have the power to walk out their destinies fearlessly.

Weenies Into Warriors

Never have I once, in all my years of going to church, ever heard a sermon about the eleven disciples that stayed in the boat after Peter decided to step out on the water and walk to Jesus. That's most likely where I would have been: with the other eleven, afraid I was seeing a ghost as well. And even brave Peter only managed a couple of steps before he was overcome by his own fear. At least he tried.

The disciples were normal, average men. They had not grown up accustomed to healings and miracles and exorcisms. Jesus completely rocked their world. As they walked with him, their confidence grew, but throughout the Gospels and even up until the point of the cross, we see all of them plagued with fear and doubt. In the end, in Jesus' greatest hour of need, they denied and abandoned him. But Jesus didn't give up on them.

After three days in the tomb, Jesus returns to find his disciples hiding out. He shows them his hands and feet and side, convinces them that, again, he's not a ghost (I don't know why this is their go-to). They make him prove it by eating something. A few short scenes later and Jesus heads back to Heaven, telling them not to do anything until they have been "clothed with power from on high" or as the New Living Translation says, "until the Holy Spirit comes and fills you with power from Heaven." In other words, please don't touch anything until you have my Spirit.

You see, the disciples didn't have the ability to self-help their way into more faith. They didn't "grow" in faith as they walked with Jesus. I mean, maybe they did a little, but not enough to stick around when he was put on trial, and definitely not enough to believe that he was actually going to come back to life again. *The Holy Spirit is the crux.* Without him, the disciples would have most likely gone back to living their lives as they did before they met Jesus.

The Holy Spirit changed everything!

We cannot expect to walk out a life of faith if we do not have God's Spirit within us. *We must be transformed.* It's true that we become more and more like Jesus over time, but that is because the Holy Spirit is at work within us. If our lives are not connected to him, it is merely striving. The *Holy Spirit* is the only way that twelve doubting weenies could possibly have metamorphosed into the mighty warriors that we read about in the Book of Acts, each of whom ended up in martyrdom for the very Lord that they once abandoned.

We must have the Holy Spirit.

Without him, we are nothing. We must be made into new creations and receive new hearts before we can begin to live out new destinies. Otherwise, we will always struggle with the same besetting sins. Even after we receive him, we must keep in step with him, but it's in the initial arrival that our lives our changed.

Just as we receive our salvation in faith, we can ask for and receive the indwelling of the Holy Spirit *in faith.* Some people are tangibly and obviously changed in an instant. For others, it's a slow growing awareness that there is a new Love at work within them. It doesn't really matter to me how he comes, but come he must! Jesus promised us this in Luke 11:

> *"'So I say to you: Ask and it will be given to you; seek and you will find; knock and the door will be opened to you. For everyone who asks receives; the one who seeks finds; and to the one who knocks, the door will be opened. Which of you fathers, if your son asks for a fish, will give him a snake instead? Or if he asks for an egg, will give him a scorpion? If you then, though you are evil, know how to give good gifts to your children, how much more will your Father in heaven give the Holy Spirit to those who ask him!'"*

If you are struggling to find what you need, whether it be faith or hope or peace or compassion or just some kind of *help*, ask the Holy Spirit. God wants you to have his Spirit more than you do. He has been drawing you to this moment since time began. It is the ultimate, eternal reason that Jesus came to earth, died on the cross and was raised back to life: so that we could once again be in unbroken communion with the Father. Once again, we become a part of his family. We are invited into the love and power of the Trinity. Do I understand this fully? By all means, no. But I believe it, and I have experienced it time and time again.

All of the wisdom, provision, protection, faith, strength, power and love that you need resides within the Helper. God is the author of our faith, and God is the perfecter of it as well.

Chapter Two

FAITH COMES BY HEARING

"Great communication begins with connection."

Oprah Winfrey

Born Communicators

The Bible tells us in Daniel 11:32, "Those who know their God will be strong and accomplish great feats." Those who *know* their God will accomplish great feats. We must know God if we expect to move the mountains that are in our path. Faith is trust, and trust comes from knowing someone well enough to believe that they will do what they say they will do. In order to trust God, in order to have faith, we must believe that he is real and that he will do what he says he will do (Hebrews 11:6).

So how do we get to know God? As humans, we get to know each other by communicating: talking, sharing, crying and laughing together. We get to know God in the same way. God is a communicator. We were made in his image, so we are communicators too. It is the principal manner in which we connect with each other. In order to have a relationship with God, we must have a means to connect with him. God wants to speak to us, and he does- even if we don't always realize it (just read Samuel's story in the Bible!)

We were designed to be in unison with God. It should be natural and normal to commune with him. It was normal in the Garden of Eden, and it should be normal now since Jesus has righted our broken relationship with the Father. In fact, it should be easier now because we have the Holy Spirit to help us. Jesus himself said that it's to our advantage that he went back to Heaven and sent the Holy Spirit in his place (John 16:7). Now we have access 24/7 to the Spirit of God.

You may be wondering if this is real or even if this is Biblical. In fact, it's nearly impossible to read the Bible without running into someone communicating with God. From Adam to Hagar to Moses to Mary, the book is full of God speaking to people and of people speaking back to him. It is 100 percent Biblical. And once the Holy Spirit enters the picture in the New Testament, there seems to be no limit the communication between people and God.

In all seasons of life, it's important to have God's perspective, but in times of crisis, it is critical that we are able to hear from God *for ourselves*. This is where faith is born. Romans 10:17 tells us, "Faith comes by hearing and hearing by the word of Christ." Without God's guiding word and his personal wisdom for us, we can be tossed about like a wave on the sea (James 1:6). Well-meaning friends and family will offer all kinds of advice, some of it medically sound and some of it straight from the latest story on Dateline.

Depending on our situation, doctors and teachers and lawyers may tell us what we should and should not do. And we should listen to their counsel; that is wisdom. However, if we want to know the steps that we should take for our specific situation, then we must hear from the Lord first and foremost. His word will bring the peace and clarity that we need. God's instructions are meant to protect us. If we follow them, our lives will be built on a strong foundation.

Jesus tells us a story in Matthew 7 of two men who build their homes on different types of ground. One builds on the sand and one on the rock. When the storms come, only the house on the rock stands. Jesus said that the man who listen to his words and *does* them is like the wise man who builds his house on the rock.

When I first announced to friends and family that I had been diagnosed with cancer, I heard all kinds of responses, depending on their theology and philosophy on life. Most said they would pray for me. Some declared that I would be healed. Others prayed for God's will to be done. Some sent me good thoughts and vibes. Others told me that homemade juice would cure me. Some encouraged me to do chemo. Others said chemo would cripple me. Some shared testimonies of loved one who were healed from cancer. Others told me how their grandmothers died from it.

All of the advice was offered in love and I appreciated the support behind each comment (even though I probably didn't need to know about the grandmas dying bit). At the end of the day though, I could not make my decisions based on the well-meaning advice of loved ones. Ultimately, I could not even rely on what the medical professionals *alone* were saying, as they would sometimes differ in their opinions.

It was crucial for me to hear from God personally about my diagnosis. I needed to take all of the advice and the counsel of doctors and family members back to God and get his perspective on it. And God was so gracious to me. Even before we knew the lump in my breast was cancerous, he preemptively whispered to my spirit one night as I was driving home that he was going to get glory from this. He said that he was going to part the waters for me. And I believed Him.

But let me remind you that this wasn't my first rodeo. I had been talking to and hearing from God for many years, so I recognized his voice when it came. I had already gotten to know him and was able to trust what he said because he had shown his faithfulness to me over the years. I have found there really is no replacement in my life for hearing God's voice.

Logos and Rhema Words

There are many Biblical examples of how we can hear from God. The Bible is one of the most powerful and most common ways that we as followers of Jesus (or anyone for that matter) can hear from God. There are two primary Greek words used in the scriptures that, when translated into English, are both written simply as *word*. The first Greek word is *logos*.[1] *Logos* refers to the total inspired Word of God and to Jesus, who is the "Living Word." The second Greek word is *rhema*. I will discuss rhema in a minute, but for now, let's look at how incredible this logos is!

The Bible was written over a 1,500 year span by 40 different authors. Unlike other religious writings, the Bible is an account of real events, places, people, and dialogue.[2] The Bible also passes many tests that any historical document must go through in order to prove its authenticity. I won't go into all of them here, but a good book to read on the subject is *The Case for Christ* by Lee Strobel. The Bible points us to God. Through it, we understand what he is like and what he values. We can see how he demonstrates his love for mankind. We can understand his eternal plan and how he desires for us to live our lives.

Through the Bible, God gives us a standard that is above and beyond humanity's wisdom. In 2 Timothy 3:16-17 it says, "All scripture is God-breathed and is useful for teaching, rebuking, correcting, and training in righteousness." Loren Cunningham's *The Book that Transforms Nations* gives multiple examples of countries that went from being rife with internal struggle and poverty to being nations of peace and prosperity simply by applying the principles of the Bible. God gave us both spiritual and physical laws. If we follow them, we will find all that we need.

The Bible also gives us a blueprint for government, education, sciences, the arts, family- in fact, all spheres of society can and should be understood through the lens of God's Word. Landa Cope's book *The Old Testament Template* is an excellent read for more insight into this. God's people should be ahead of their time in all walks of life because they are connected to divine knowledge.

The *rhema* word is different to *logos*. It is God's personal, specific, in-season word to us. He may highlight a verse or portion of Scripture in such a way that we know it is his *customized* word for us at that particular moment. The Greek word *rhema* literally means "utterance." It is the Holy Spirit giving utterance to the written Word.

Countless times in my life, I have come to my daily time with God and heard personally from him through the Scriptures. He may answer one of my questions or give assurance to whatever concern is on my heart. God has used the Bible to bring anything from encouragement to rebuke into my life. (I do prefer the encouragement, but alas, I need the correction as well. And even his correction is so kind!)

Even though I've read through the Bible many times, the Holy Spirit continues to highlight certain verses or passages in new ways that I have never seen before. A few years ago, I was asking God (and fretting) about our financial situation. As I spent time reading his Word, I came across these words in Isaiah 46:4, words that brought tears of conviction and relief because I was again reminded that God would take care of me:

"Even to your old age and gray hairs I am he, I am he who will sustain you. I have made you and I will carry you; I will sustain you and I will rescue you."

As we read his *logos* Word and hear his *rhema* word, it becomes our daily bread. Jesus himself declares that *he* is the Word[3] in flesh and the Bread of life[4]. God's word may come in the form of Scripture, of Jesus himself, or in the *rhema* word of God, quickened to us by the Holy Spirit. He is such a good God! And he so loves to chat with his kids!

This is one reason why it is so important to spend time in the Word. Not only will the Holy Spirit speak to us as we are actually reading the Bible, but the more we know it, the more he is able to remind us of its truth throughout the day. Like the little squirrels who destroy my garden in the fall, burying their nuts in the soil for the upcoming winter, we must bury God's Word in our hearts in times of plenty so that we can access it during the lean seasons of life.

"For the word of God is alive and active. Sharper than any double-edged sword, it penetrates even dividing soul and spirit, joints and marrow; it judges the thoughts and attitudes of the heart."
Hebrews 4:12

The Word is *living*. We don't read the Bible so that we can check it off our religious chore list. We are investing time into our relationship with Jesus. The Psalms say that God shares his secrets with those who fear him.[5] The point is not merely to read it for reading's sake but to find and know the God of those pages. The Bible is full of God's promises to us. We can stand on those promises because of the One who spoke them. He is faithful. He can be tested and proven true.

Spirit, Lead Me

I spent my entire childhood hearing from God through both forms of his Word: *logos* and *rhema,* but it wasn't until I learned to recognize the voice of the Holy Spirit within my own being that my relationship with God really began to grow to new levels of intimacy.

I believe that this type of close friendship through intimate communication with his Spirit is the original way that God wanted to relate to mankind. We see him speaking to Adam and Eve. We see him calling Abraham into a new land. We see him discussing many matters with Moses. And now because of Jesus, we *all* can have access to this kind of intimate relationship with the Father. This is what he has always wanted. You can hear his heart cry in Psalm 81:13, "Oh, that my people would listen to me! Oh that Israel would follow me."

When Jesus walked on this earth, he was still limited by a physical body. He was only able to be in one place at any given time. The Holy Spirit does not have this limitation. The Holy Spirit is with us all of the time because he dwells within us. He is always ready to comfort, teach, direct, instruct, help, correct-whatever you need.

He loves to speak to us in that "still, small voice." He gives wisdom when we ask for it just like he promised to in James 1:5. He gives discernment when we are unclear about what is really going on in a situation like Hebrews 5:14 explains. And he brings light into areas of darkness like he did for Daniel in the Book of Daniel chapter 2.

Many times in the Bible, we see people being led by the Holy Spirit in this way. In the Old Testament, only a select few were led personally by the Spirit of God. In the New Testament, our supreme model, Jesus receives the Holy Spirit after being baptized and is then "led by the Holy Spirit into the desert."[6]

Upon Jesus' return to Heaven, the Holy Spirit comes upon those of his followers who were gathered in the Upper Room. We can see that after Jesus' death, resurrection, and ascension, the

28

playing field is leveled. The curtain was torn in two; all who believe in Jesus can receive the Holy Spirit. As 1 John 2:27 states:

"As for you, the anointing you received from him remains in you, and you do not need anyone to teach you. But as his anointing teaches you about all things and as that anointing is real, not counterfeit- just as it has taught you, remain in him."

It's not that we no longer need teachers to help us understand the Word or the ways of God, but that we no longer have to rely *solely* on other people to hear the voice of God.

After ten years in China, my husband, Rich, and I, along with our two small children, relocated to Cambodia. We either gave away or sold almost everything we had and boarded a flight to Phnom Penh. We were staying in cheap hotels, hoping and praying that God would open up a place for us to live. Nothing was happening, and I was getting desperate trying to entertain and care for a two-year-old toddler and a six-month-old baby in a small, tiled room.

Around day 14, I put our baby girl down for her nap and took some time to ask the Lord if there was any specific direction that he had for us. All that came to mind was a name: Sophia. I could have written it off as some random thought, but I have learned along the way not to ignore that small voice. I googled "real estate agent Phnom Penh Sophia" and a man's name, phone number, and property listings popped up. (Apparently, Sophea is a male's name in Cambodia.) Anyway, to make a long story short, we ended up renting a comfortable and safe home through…you guessed it, Real Estate Agent Sophea!

At other times, instead of hearing God speak into our hearts, it's almost as though we can *sense* what he is saying. It's as if we know what we are meant to do before we fully understand it with our logical minds. This happened to my husband and I while we were on furlough in my hometown in Colorado after many years overseas on the mission field. We had been under the impression that we were meant to leave Colorado shortly and move onto our next assignment, but details were just not falling into place as we had hoped.

We kept taking our situation back to the Lord in prayer and one day, Rich just "knew" that we were meant to continue on in Colorado until our circumstances shifted. I can't describe what changed his mind or why he came to that conclusion. It was as though something was just *illuminated* for him and what he previously could not see, he now did. When he shared this new idea with me, it didn't take long until I had the same confirmation within my own spirit. A *sense* that yes, this was the right step.

It's hard to find the language for this type of leading because in our modern societies, we so rarely rely on our spirits (which are now indwelt by the Holy Spirit if we are followers of Jesus) to direct us. Most of us in the West have been educated in the Greek way of thinking which is to rely almost entirely on our minds. Even though this type of leading by the Spirit is *extremely common* in the Bible, we may find it hard to get past our own worldview. And many wise and well-meaning Christian teachers only serve to enforce these faulty thought patterns.

If you're not used to keeping in step with the Spirit in this manner, it will most likely feel strange at first. That is not necessarily because it is wrong but because it is *new*. I recommend you start out leaning in to hear him over smaller matters at first. When I first began learning to hear God in this way, I often asked him to give me words for other people or situations, encouragement that I could share. Even though I felt very timid, I would do my best to step out and share those words to see if I was hearing from God correctly or not.

I remember one time while journaling in a coffee shop I noticed a woman who was sweeping the floor. Upon seeing her, I immediately felt that I should approach her and tell her that God "sees" her. I presumed that this thought was from God because I would not want to do this in my natural, introverted self and I'm sure the enemy would not want me to encourage someone else either.

I felt very intimidated, but I agreed to step out on this hunch from God. I walked up to the lady and stammered out something like, "Um, this might sound kind of strange, but um, I'm a Christian, and um, I feel like God wanted me to tell you that he sees you, and that he loves you." Awkward silence. Once the woman took in what I was saying, a huge smile broke out on her face, and she gave me a big hug. She repeatedly thanked me as I shyly gathered my belongings and headed for the door.

Our kids can learn to hear from God directly as well. Before my son was due to start kindergarten, I was nervous. Our son was a little nervous too. I was trying not be nervous so that he would not be nervous, but I still was! I told myself that God had got this and that he would help us both, but it was still hard to shake the jitters.

One morning, our son awoke and said he had a dream. He believed that it was from God. He told us that in the dream, there was a river with lots of alligators in it. There were also some big rocks. He and I were jumping across the river on the rocks, and I was very relieved to hear that in the dream, we made it to the other side! We asked him what he thought God was trying to say to him and he said, "God is telling me that even though there's some scary parts about starting kindergarten, Mama and I are going to get to the other side okay."

The dream had comforted him, but I wonder if God knew that the dream would comfort me even more. I wasn't always going to be there with him. I couldn't hold his hand and make everything okay. I couldn't give him all the answers, but God could. God was showing us both that he can speak directly to my kids (and get us to the other side of the river safely!). The Holy Spirit is just as much the Comforter, Healer, and Teacher for our children as he is for us.

As we walk on this path of learning to hear God speak, we will most likely make mistakes, but if we continue to ask the Holy Spirit to guide us like this in small decisions, the consequences of hearing incorrectly shouldn't be too grave. I remember one time as I was praying for God to heal me as I recovered from an injury, the thought came into my head that I should get on my children's tree swing as a step of faith that I could begin to do normal activities again. I was nervous because I hadn't done much more than limp from the kitchen to the bedroom for the past couple of weeks, but I decided that I would try it. I made it out to the backyard and over to the tree swing. I even managed to straddle the rope with no event, but when I put my full weight on the swing and lifted my legs up, the rope broke! I fell on my tooshie and then the rope hit me in the face. I don't think that I really had heard from God that time, but he probably got a good chuckle out of it. Fortunately nothing was hurt, other than my pride.

The more that we learn to distinguish God's voice from our own, the more confident we will become in stepping out on what he says. I like the example that I heard once about how we need to "tune in" to the Spirit's voice. He is speaking, but if we don't have our "radios" dialed in to his frequency, we will miss what he's saying. The more time we spend listening to him, the more accustomed we will become to how he speaks. Remember, John 10 tells us that we are his sheep and *we hear his voice*. Shepherds generally want to lead their sheep more than their sheep want to be led, so fear not!

A Manner of Speaking

There are various other Biblical examples of ways that God uses to speak to people. The Holy Spirit is extremely humble, and I have noticed that he generally speaks to us in the way that we think we can hear from him. If our vein of Christianity says that we can only hear God through the Bible, then he speaks through the Bible. If our church teaches that God speaks mostly through dreams and visions, I see a lot more people hearing from God at night. God can speak any way he wants to. I have heard accounts from Muslim brothers and sisters who were praying to know the truth in their mosques during the season of Ramadan when Jesus revealed himself to them personally. God is not limited by our rules or traditions!

I'll just throw out a few more ways that the Bible teaches us how God speaks:

1) Through Other People

The Bible is full of examples where God uses other people to get his point across. In Acts 5, Peter receives a word of knowledge about what Ananias and Sapphira are really up to. In Acts 21, Agabus tells Paul that if he goes to Rome, there will be chains waiting there for him.

Before I became a missionary, I remember a woman praying for me at a Christian conference that I attended. She told me that she felt she should pray over my feet! She said that they would go into many nations. Her word has proven true. God has taken my feet (and the rest of me) into many nations. The Holy Spirit revealed that to her so that she could pray for and encourage me.

God can also use people to speak to us in more indirect ways. If you've ever heard your pastor speak on a Sunday morning and felt the prompting of the Holy Spirit, you know what I'm talking about. He can use a seemingly "random" story from a friend, a well-timed phone call, or a much needed blog post from someone who seems to have read your mail. God can and does use all of these ways to speak to us.

2) Through Creation

Creation reveals God. In Psalm 19:1-3, we read, "The heavens declare the glory of God; the skies proclaim the works of his hands. Day after day they pour forth speech; night after night they display knowledge. There is no speech or language where their voice is not heard." This is a common and often a very overlooked way that God speaks to us.

It is so easy to walk outside and miss all that God is saying. But everything that God has created is expressing some facet about him. Just as every word you write, every picture you take, and everything that you create expresses something about you. How much more does God's creation do the same for him?

In fact, the voice of creation is such a powerful way that God uses to display his eternal power and divine nature that Paul says we are without excuse if we fail to heed its call.[7] In Job 12:7-10 we read:

"Ask the animals, and they will teach you, or the birds of the air, and they will tell you; or speak to the earth, and it will teach you, or let the fish of the sea inform you. Which of these does not know that the hand of the Lord has done this? In his hand is the life of every creature and the breath of all mankind."

Albert Einstein said, "I believe in God- who reveals himself in the orderly harmony of the universe." And Sir Isaac Newton is quoted saying, "In the absence of any other proof, the thumb alone would convince me of God's presence."

In watching the transformative growth of an acorn into a large oak tree, we can understand that we should not despise a small beginning. We must all start small and grow into what we are meant to be. By witnessing the sun rise and set daily, we can see God's faithfulness. He will do what he has promised. And by watching the four seasons come and go each year, we can understand that there is a time for every activity under heaven. God gives space and boundaries to all.

Just recently God was speaking to me through the little birds that visit the bushes outside of our home. There is a bold, flashy cardinal and a simple, shy sparrow. They are so different, but both are lovely. Through their presence, God was reminding me that every creature gives God glory simply by being themselves. I was reminded that I don't have to fit into someone else's mold of what it takes to be a good _____ (mother/wife/daughter/woman/teacher/missionary/etc). All I have to be is who he made me to be. That is what brings him pleasure and displays his glory the most.

3) Through Dreams, Visions, and Angels

In many parts of the world, it is still quite normal to hear from God through dreams and visions and even witness angels. I hope it will continue to increase in the Western world as well. There are many times in the Old Testament where people hear from God in one of these ways, but I will draw examples from the New Testament, since the times in which we now live are A.D.

Jesus Himself was ministered to by angels in Matthew 4:11. Peter and an angel made a jailbreak in Acts 12. Cornelius, the Roman Centurion received a message from an angel in Acts 10. Peter had a vision that helped to convince him that all food is now kosher in Acts 10. John wrote the entire book of Revelation through a vision. And Paul went to Macedonia after receiving direction in a dream in Acts 16.

I rarely hear from God this way, but one of the earliest times that I remember hearing from him as a child was actually in a dream. I was about 10 years old, and some of my classmates and I had gotten into an argument at school. I came home and was very distressed about the break in relationship. I couldn't stop worrying about it and was very nervous to return to school to see them. I remember waking from my sleep the next morning with a dream: my classmates and I were all sitting in a big circle and were happy. It was a very simple dream, but I felt that it was encouragement from God that everything would be okay. And everything turned out just as he showed me in my dream.

I am not saying that every dream we have is from God, but there is a certain *weight* to the dreams that are. God is able to confirm to us the dreams that are from him as well. When in doubt, ask him about it and seek out wise counsel.

Visions are different than dreams. A vision is generally referred to as a picture that we see while we are awake. A dream occurs while we are asleep. I can remember only one significant vision that I have ever had and it was probably because the direction that came through this vision would have profound consequence in my life. In 2003, I felt that God was calling me to move to China as a missionary. I had just finished a degree in Spanish Bilingual Education and had no humanly draw towards Asia. It was a huge decision, and I really needed to know that I was hearing from God.

One day, as I was sitting in a class, I saw in my mind's eye, but with my eyes *open*, a picture of a large red flag with a yellow symbol in the top left corner. I'm sorry to say that I didn't even know *for sure* if this was China's flag or not. Obviously, geography was not my strong point. Once I discovered that yes, China's flag was in fact red with a yellow symbol in the top left corner, I strongly felt that this was God's confirmation to me. I was meant to go to China as a missionary.

4) Through Our Circumstances

We see the way that God uses circumstances to speak to people very clearly illustrated in the story of Elisha at the brook in 1 Kings 17. There was famine in Israel. God had led the prophet Elisha to a brook. Everyday, God would send ravens to feed Elisha bread, and he would drink from the brook. After some time passed, the brook dried up. The Bible clarifies that this was God's way of moving Elisha on. Then God gave him directions for what his next step was to be.

In a similar fashion, God tried to use Jonah's circumstances at the end of the book of Jonah to soften his heart. God caused a vine to grow and offered Jonah shade. Then God caused a worm to come and eat the vine. Jonah wasn't too happy about God's teaching methods, but they were effective!

It can be hard at times to let go of a person, place, or thing *especially* if it was God who provided it for us in the first place! But if we try to hold on to what God is moving us away from, we can end up camped out by a dry riverbed, complaining to God because he isn't providing!

When seasons begin to shift in our lives, we need to ask God if the change is coming from him or not. Not all obstacles are from God. Some can be from other people and their choices. Some can be from the enemy of our souls and should be dealt with accordingly. But if the obstacles are from God, we need to recognize them for what they are and agree with what God is doing. If we dig in our heels, we will only find ourselves kicking against the goads.

Richard and I found this happening to us while we were living in Cambodia. We knew that God had called us to step out of China even though we had been living there for ten years and were very committed to the work. We felt that the next step was to move to Cambodia, but once we were there, life did not happen as we had planned.

It was as if *every* door that we tried to walk through was not just locked but also dead-bolted. We reached out to many ministries and NGOs and churches, looking for a place to connect with and get involved, but nothing materialized. After two or three months of trying, finally *one* small church made room for my husband to minister with them. But within a month, the pastor called and said that the church had split and they would no longer be meeting!?!

We didn't know what was going on. We went back to God and began to (slowly) realize that *he* was behind the closed doors. In hindsight, we can see that he had called us to step out of China and into Cambodia so that he could eventually lead us to be based out of the U.S. for the next season of our lives. We wouldn't have been able to hear his instructions to leave Asia if we were still living in China. We had invested too much. Living in that part of the world was all that we knew and were able to even consider at the time. God had to take us out of ourselves, out of our "normal" to bring us to a place where we could hear the *bigger picture* of what he was saying. He used our circumstances to speak to us.

God also used Mary and Joseph's circumstances to speak to them. It just so *happened* that a census was called for at the very same time that Mary was about to have baby Jesus. They could have resisted what the Roman government was demanding that they do. They could have decided to rage against the machine and go hide in the hills. But they agreed with life's demands and traveled to Bethlehem, unknowingly fulfilling a prophecy about where the Messiah would be born.

God is always at work. He is working out your life for your good. Even if He's not directly *causing* everything that happens to us, we can be sure that he is orchestrating it for our good. He can even use the government to accomplish his will!

God won't force himself upon us. He is a gentleman. He waits until we are ready to turn to him and listen, but make no mistake, he wants to have a relationship with us. He wants to speak to us and listen to what we have to say. There is only one of you in all of the universe. Just as my son brings me a different pleasure than my daughter because they are different people, so you bring a unique joy to the heart of God.

(A great resource for principles in learning to hear God's voice is Joy Dawson's book *Forever Ruined for the Ordinary*. My ability to hear from God was transformed by applying the wisdom from her teaching. Another great resource is *Translating God* by Shawn Bolz. He has some awesome stories of hearing from God for other people. You can also download a free copy of my book *7 Biblical Ways to Hear God's Voice* on my website www.brookegrangard.com).

Chapter Three

WHY DOES IT HAVE TO BE SO HARD?

"Life is not always fair. Sometimes you get a splinter sliding down a rainbow."

Terri Guillemets

Trouble is Promised

When I was about nine years old, a friend and I convinced our parents to let us go away to a weeklong Christian summer camp in the foothills outside of Denver. They thought we were a little too young, but we very persistently presented our case and eventually won them over. We had dreams of campfire songs and horseback rides dancing in our heads and would not be deterred. But when we arrived at the camp, we soon discovered that its reality did not match our imaginations.

The seven days I spent at that camp made up one terrible, horrible, no good, very bad week. Because my friend and I were amongst the younger campers, we were quickly demoted to

41

sleeping on the top bunks. Colorado nights are cool in the mountains even in the summertime, so I brought my footed zip-up pajamas like any naive nine-year-old would do. One night, whilst sitting on the edge of the bed with my legs dangling down, the older girls below seized my footed jammies and pulled me down into their bullies' lair. I was humiliated.

The next morning, my friend and I were falsely accused of destroying the popular girls' carefully designed rock formations- I'm sure they were in the image of the cross or something else very Christian. We were then sentenced to clean the girls' camp bathroom (this was 1989, when child labor was still permissible).

Halfway through the week, my friend got sick and spent the rest of the time in the nurse's quarters, so I suffered through the remaining camp's activities in solitude. This included an intense, twilight game of Capture the Flag where I was so nervous hiding out in the woods that I didn't dare take a bathroom break and instead peed my pants. This I had to report to my camp counselor and then proceed to wander back alone in silent shame to the cabins to change into clean pants.

But the cherry on the top of the world's longest week was what happened on one of the last nights. It was gospel presentation night, so all of the kids from the entire camp were sitting out on a beautiful hillside overlooking the Rockies. The speaker had been building up to this evening all week long and was finally ready to share the eternal good news of our Lord and Savior Jesus Christ. Every child sat miraculously still and listened intently, but it was not the good news that they heard next. It was the rumble of a loud and long gassy wind coming from my hindquarters.

Yes, it's true. This was THE most embarrassing moment of my nine years on earth. Once the sound was dropped, children everywhere began to turn and look for the culprit. In panic, I did the same, hoping that no one would notice who the guilty party was. No such luck. As I swiveled my head to look behind me, the boy seated directly in my path knew that there could be no other. "It was her," he cried and pointed his chubby little finger in my direction.

I have no recollection of what happened after those words. Did the speaker finish his talk? Did we pray or respond to the message? Did we sit on the hill or have s'mores after? I have no idea. I was consumed only with my own flatulence and the shame that I had brought upon myself. Needless to say, I was never more grateful to see my mom's Jeep pulling in to pick me up at the end of that long, tortuous week.

Life is hard. It is not all sugar plums and gum drops. You think you're getting hours of camp time fun when really all you're getting is sad little crafts and your own bodily functions going rogue. Some of the troubles in life we bring on ourselves, and others are brought upon us. This world is broken (and apparently so was my lower intestine). We are guaranteed hardship. Jesus promised us in John 16:33, "In this world you will have trouble." Thanks, JC, that's comforting. The *actual* comforting part of that statement is what follows it: "but take heart, I have overcome the world."

When sin entered the world, everything was thrown off kilter. We lost our true north. The door to brokenness was opened, and we have not recovered since. Jesus came to set the world right, and that he has. His Kingdom trumps the kingdom of darkness, but the two are still both at work in this realm. Pain and sickness and addiction and persecution and loss and poverty and greed and racism and pride. The list goes on and on. Death followed sin, and the symptoms of death are found in humanity's crippled reality.

For over 16 weeks straight, I traveled almost weekly to the largest hospital in Colorado to have chemotherapy treatments. The building east of the cancer wing is the Denver Children's Hospital. It is a massive structure with countless rooms and billions of dollars worth of equipment inside to treat all of the sickness and pain that children face in our area. I am grateful to live in a country that has such facilities, but as my husband and I drove past one particular day, a deep anger within me rose up, and I cried out in anguish and rage that I couldn't wait for Jesus to return and burn it all up. The response startled Rich because it was in such direct contrast to the lite seventies rock that we were listening to on the radio, and he wasn't quite sure that Jesus would be burning anything up upon his return, but I think he grasped my sentiment.

There is a grief and a righteous anger in the heart of God (and so in our hearts) because of this broken state in which we daily find ourselves. Jesus set it right through his death and resurrection, and we *can* see healing and hope here on earth, but it will not be fully renewed until he returns and brings the new earth with him. How do people live without the hope of heaven? What sweet, sweet news it is.

One day, we will have no need for a cancer ward or a children's hospital because no one will be sick. Our new bodies won't have malfunctioning genes and our joints won't wear out. Our hearts won't be broken nor our hopes dashed. He will wipe every tear from our eyes. No more death or sickness or pain. All will be restored. All will be whole for all will be holy, as it was meant to be. On earth as it is in heaven.

That is the promise of our coming reality, so why can't it just *be here* already? What good can come of pain? Perhaps some can.

As I write the following words, I want to be very clear that I do not believe that God causes pain to punish us for sin. I believe that Jesus took our punishment on the cross. I don't think that God would punish us for the same sin for which he punished Jesus. That would be unjust. God *disciplines* us in his love and allows us to feel the consequence of our own choices. This does account for the some of the pain that we encounter.

I also believe in an enemy whose full intention is to steal from us, kill us, and destroy us like Jesus pointed out in the tenth chapter of John. He hates our Father, and he hates us. He will do everything in his power to harm God's creation. This is no little red cartoon character with horns and a pitchfork. This is a fallen angel who is bent on devouring us. Much of the pain in this world can ultimately be traced back to him.

If we have no framework or theology for a devil, we can easily be taken advantage of. If this is new to you or you have doubts, welcome to the club. I don't understand it all either. But check out the way that Jesus lived and how he interacted with the spiritual realm when he dealt with the demonic. Jesus is God in the flesh. I'm sure he understands best how both the physical and spiritual world operate. Either he was really driving out demons or he was mentally unsound. I believe the former is true, but I'll write more about that in a bit.

Another reason we experience pain is because of free will. We argue amongst each other because we can. My children are a prime example of this when they fight about a leftover toy that one of them received from the last fast food joint that we visited. No one has played with this toy in over a month but because one of them *rediscovered* it, it is now the most valuable possession in the whole house.

God is not out to harm us. He is for us. He has good plans and wants to prosper us (Jeremiah 29:11). We can harm ourselves. The devil can harm us. And others can harm us. God doesn't have to wait long for pain to occur. It's all over the place. He does, however, use the pain to grow us, to teach us, and even to strengthen us. In short, he uses it for our good (Romans 8:28). There was pain from my surgery to remove the cancer and there was pain in the physical therapy to regain full use of the muscles that were damaged, but both of those pains were ultimately to help me.

God could protect us from all pain, but he doesn't. He is more often referred to as our *Deliverer* than our *Protector* in the Bible. So let's look at the different kinds of pain and how God can use them to prosper us.

1) The Pain We Give Ourselves

Basically, this is the hardship that we bring on ourselves for dumb things that we do. "If only I checked myself," says the guy who wrecked himself. We get mad at our spouses for leaving dirty socks on the bathroom floor and say something snarky which causes a rift in the relationship, and then we feel lonely that evening because our spouses don't want to hang out with us. By "we" I mean "me".

There are countless examples of this in my own life, and I think we are all intelligent enough to understand this kind of pain without an anecdotal parable. Most of the pain in my life I bring on myself. If I could just keep my mouth shut when I should, my life would probably be ninety-nine percent smoother than it is now. As a kid, this was my problem as well. As a grown woman, I continue to "reap what I sow." Some habits die hard. I have grown in this area, so it is better than before (thank you, Jesus), but I'm still my own worst enemy.

God doesn't have to do much to use this kind of pain to teach us. The consequence of disobedience and foolishness is painful enough in itself. If you put hot coals in your lap, you'll get burnt. The unfortunate part is how stuck we can get in our own sin. Thankfully we have a Savior. There are times though when we don't even realize that we've taken a wrong turn. Pride and ignorance can blind us to what we are doing. We can miss the caution signs along the way either in deception or in willful neglect. Whichever way, we end up headed for a cliff. It's at these times that pain can be our greatest ally. God may even bring pain *to protect* us from destroying ourselves.

C.S. Lewis says this in *The Problem with Pain:*

> *The human spirit will not even begin to try to surrender*
> *self-will as long as all seems to be well with it. Now error and*
> *sin both have this property, that the deeper they are, the less*
> *their victim suspects their existence; they are masked evil. Pain*
> *is unmasked, unmistakable evil; every man knows that*
> *something is wrong when he is being hurt.*

We might not realize where we are headed when we set out boldly on our own stubborn path, but God does. He will

47

graciously allow pain to accompany the fruit of our bad choices in hopes that it will awaken us to the danger that lies ahead. I heard it once compared to a man standing in the middle of the street at the bottom of an icy hill trying to stop oncoming traffic because just around the bend, the road has given out. The man's behavior was annoying all the drivers until they realized just what he was trying to protect them from.

This type of pain or "annoyance" is from the hand of a loving Father leaving all the lights on in hopes that his prodigal children will feel the effect of their self-harming ways and come back home.

2) The Pain the Enemy Gives

That crafty little serpent in the Garden of Eden knew that if he could convince humans to open the door to sin, then all hell would literally break loose. Before the Fall, the Kingdom of God reigned in Eden. With Eve and Adam's choices to doubt God's goodness towards them and in turn, try to create and control their own destinies, hell entered. The door was opened for sin and thus, death. Darkness where once was only light. Yes, it's true, we have the authority to open or close the door to sinful choices in our own lives, but there is a tempter in our midst as well. We have an enemy, and we would do well to recognize.

A good question to ask is, "If I were my own worst enemy, what would I do to bring me down?" The answer to that question is most likely already abundantly clear in the broken areas of your own life. I know it is in mine. If I were my own worst enemy, I would accuse my husband of all kinds of selfishness and keep my own flaws out of the picture. I would tell myself that my children are a burden and have the power to make me feel crazy even though the truth is that no one has the power to surrender my self-control but me. I would place nagging thoughts in my head about how others are out to get me and are just thinking of themselves.

I would tell myself that I'm not good enough and try to stir up fear so that I would back down from the desires that God has placed in my heart. I would do this enough so as to work myself out of a job. Eventually it would become my default inner dialogue, and an enemy would no longer be needed.

And isn't that just how the accuser works? Accusing you, accusing your loved ones *to* you, accusing random strangers and government leaders and even citizens from other countries or people of other colors. Stirring up fear and suspicion so that we become trapped in our own little worlds. The fallout of the Fall.

Now that we can see his work in our own lives, we don't have to succumb to it anymore. The good news is that once Jesus died and rose again, he gave us the keys to take back the destinies which were stolen from us in the Garden. We can now expose the works of darkness (Ephesians 5:11), resist the devil (James 4:7), and choose to walk in the light of God's Kingdom (1 John 1:7). We have been set free from sin. We don't have to keep on sinning!

I first realized the truth of those words in college. Even though I had been walking with God since I was a child, I felt trapped in my harmful, emotionally-driven outbursts. I knew what I was doing was wrong, but I couldn't stop doing it. Whenever I was tested, I would respond in anger and rejection, hurting others and ultimately myself. It wasn't until God graciously gave me revelation from Romans and showed me that I had in fact *already* been set free from sin. I didn't have to walk in it any longer.

I had read those words many times in the past, but at that particular moment, God opened my eyes to see and understand what was being said. I was free. I didn't have to live like I was bound any longer. It was an "Aha" moment and the chains fell off. I was free to respond with self-control and peace, the way I was made to do. I still come back to those words when I'm feeling trapped in any particular response and remind myself that I am free to walk in the fruit of his Spirit. I no longer am bound by the lies of the enemy that say I have no choice.

I believe that much of what we see in the physical realm of the Old Testament, we now understand in the spiritual realm. What once was a physical nation of God became a spiritual nation when Jesus died and rose again to save all people. We see this message echoed throughout the New Testament as God shows us that it's those who follow Jesus who are truly Abraham's children. The physical battles that the nation of Israel fought to extend Yahweh's kingdom in the past are now spiritual battles that we must fight (Ephesians 6:12). Jesus changed everything, but we can still draw from the lessons that these ancient people of faith taught us.

When Israel was a young nation just starting out in the books of Genesis and Exodus and then expanding throughout David's lifetime and beyond, she had obvious enemies. There were other people who hated the Israelites and hoped to wipe them from the face of the earth. They were enslaved and attacked, deceived and killed. God raised up leaders to help them. He trained them to defend themselves and to see victory over their enemies.

In the third chapter of the Book of Judges, we see a new generation of Israelites who had not seen the mighty miracles of God throughout the pages of Exodus and had not yet fought off oncoming enemies. This interesting verse shows us a glimpse of God's heart in allowing their adversaries to remain:

> *"These are the nations **that the LORD left** in the land to test those Israelites who had not experienced the wars of Canaan. He did this to teach warfare to generations of Israelites who had no experience in battle. These are the nations: the Philistines, all the Canaanites, the Sidonians, and the Hivites living in the mountains of Lebanon from Mount Baal-hermon to Lebo-hamath.*
> *These people were left to test the Israelites- to see whether they would obey the commands the LORD had given to their ancestors through Moses."*
> Judges 3:1-4

God wanted the Israelites to prosper, to pass their tests, to learn to fight, so he *allowed their enemies to remain!* He does the same for you and I. It is no longer flesh and blood that we fight against, but we do have enemies in the spiritual realm. He could have removed them on that first Easter morning, but he did not. Even though the devil was defeated on the cross, he still has not been banished from earth. Could it be that God wants us to learn warfare along the way?

We have been given authority and do not have to helplessly surrender to whatever attack comes our way. Much of the pain and sickness and even death that we see all around us is ultimately inspired by our enemy. We do not have to stand for it. God will allow us to face more than we can handle on our own, but he does not allow more than we can handle *with his help.*

51

With him, we can do all things (Philippians 4:13). He is a God of miracles, a God of breakthrough (2 Samuel 5:20). In Jesus, we see the image of the invisible God (Colossians 1:15). We see provision in scarcity (Matthew 14), dominion over nature (Mark 4), authority over sickness and disease (every Gospel written), power to drive out the demonic, and wisdom for all circumstances (James 1:5). There is nothing that we will face that together with Jesus we won't be able to handle. Period. We might not believe it or feel it, but that is the truth. Either he is who he says he is, or he's a liar.

Jesus gave us authority to do these works and more (John 14:12). Some may say that was a thing of the past, only for his disciples and no one else, but there is *no indication* of this in the Bible. And there are countless testimonies from around the world, in generations past and up until this present moment, of God doing the impossible for those who asked him and believed him to do it.

In much of the non-Western world, it it normal to believe, operate in, and even engage with the spiritual realm, whether that be for good or evil. It is not as big of a stretch for most of the world to believe in a God who does supernatural acts because *they've already experienced the supernatural.* In fact, this is a much more wholistic way to live life. True, not every bad thing that happens is from the devil. In no way do I believe that. Not every sickness or oppression or mental health issue is due to a demon...but some are. Don't worry, it makes me uncomfortable too. But it's so clear in the way that Jesus operated that it simply can not be ignored. It also didn't seem to matter too much to Jesus if that problem was rooted in the physical or spiritual, he corrected them both with one command!

We don't need to get all worked up about how to deal with every circumstance that comes our way or discern the root of every problem. And we don't even need to scream or shout. It doesn't matter if a cop is loud or quiet, her authority is just the same! If you sense that the problem could be spiritual, just try commanding any demonic influence to leave in Jesus name. If that deals with it, then you know that it was a spiritual issue! If it doesn't, pray for healing. If that doesn't fix it, ask God for wisdom for the next step and proceed from there, trusting that he will give it to you when you need it. Deng Xiao Ping, China's Chairman after Mao, is famously quoted for saying, "It doesn't matter if a cat is black or white so long as it catches mice." Who cares where the problem originates from as long as Jesus can give us the answer?!

I received all kinds of spiritual and physical advice when I was diagnosed with cancer. This advice came from people of many different nations and denominations! Some people told me that the cancer was due to a generational curse in my family because it came down through my maternal line. Others asked if there was unforgiveness in my heart that could have opened the door to this disease. Some people told me it was because I ate chemically processed meat. Others recommended I switch to non-toxic lotion.

Which advice was right? Honestly, I don't know. I thought it best to cover my bases! But mostly, I clung to the *personal* promises that I received from the Holy Spirit in faith because I believed that he would do what he said he would do. And when I wavered in that faith, I asked him to give me more faith or bring someone alongside of me that was strong in theirs at the moment to stand with me.

There's probably better and more spiritual advice out there. And I would recommend you read it, but at the end of the day, it's going to be between you and the Lord. He will give you the wisdom that you need for each step. That wisdom may come directly through his Word. It may come through the advice of a friend. It may come in a dream. It may come through a medical article. He knows exactly what you need on your path to healing or breakthrough or whatever challenge you are facing. We must trust that he will provide what is needed for the journey.

3) The Pain Others Give

If you have not had the pleasure of befriending a native Norwegian personally, you may not realize that they are known to be incredibly loyal. They are also incredibly (and sometimes painfully) sincere. This is most likely the reason that Norway's government has a corruption rate of around zero percent. That's apparently a real thing.

This sincerity is awesome in government, but it can sometimes get them (by them, I mean my husband) into trouble. Opinions are often delivered in a very direct manner and without any "cushioning". Just recently, in a moment of insecurity with my fresh post-cancer hair growing back in unexplained ways on my head, I asked Rich if he thought I was ugly or not. (I don't know why I still ask him questions like this.) He paused and took a moment to study my face. "No," he replied, "You are not ugly. Your hair has seen better days, but you are not ugly." Um... wrong answer.

This sincerity has been a source of angst but also humor in our family. My two children are also very Norwegian in this aspect, speaking exactly what is on their mind. When I first lost my hair after chemo, my son asked me to please keep my cap on because my head looked weird. My daughter told me that my new wig made me look like Mr. Tumnus, the fawn from the movie, *The Lion, The Witch, and the Wardrobe*. And my husband also informed me that when I wore it, I looked like I was on a Saturday Night Live skit. Needless to say, the wig didn't last too long even with all of the support.

Maybe their comments did hurt my feelings a little, but mostly they made me laugh because they were right. I did look like a strange, make-believe character on an SNL episode, but I knew I could count on them to keep it real. This is an example of a very mild sort of pain that others can give us, but there is also a real and cutting pain that most of us have experienced in life at least some time or another.

This deeper kind of pain can be traced back as far as Cain and Abel. The free will of others will cause us pain. Can't live with 'em. Can't live without 'em. This pain is obvious when someone cuts you off in traffic or gossips behind your back. "God, why don't you smite them, o mighty Smiter?" In doing so, he would have to smite me as well. We are all guilty. But that doesn't take away the hurt. It is a real and certain pain. It is also the consequence of living in a world where people are free to make their own choices, whether good or bad.

Much of the pain that is inflicted by humans is blamed on God. If there were no greed or corruption, if we didn't consume more than we needed and willingly shared our excess, if we were never afraid to step out and try new ideas and were always concerned with others as much as we're concerned with ourselves, if we worked hard and were never lazy, if we took care of the planet in a better way, if we held the hardships of those caught in famine and war as if they were our own kin, would there still be poverty and desolation on the earth? My guess is that there would be much, much less.

A few days after Rich and I's honeymoon ended in May of 2008 and we returned to China, there was an 8.0 earthquake in the province in which we were living at the time. It had devastating effects on the people in the area. More than 80,000 died and an estimated 15 million homes were destroyed. We took a bus down with our team to the area most affected to help in any way that we could. The government had set up tents and was handing out provisions to those who were in need, so we helped them and gave out bottles of water, but mostly we just listened. People were desperate to tell their stories. They wanted someone to hear what had happened, what they had gone through, how much they had lost.

Oftentimes after a natural disaster such as this, one will begin to hear voices online or in person speaking of God's judgement on a people or a country. And this time was not an exception. But I also heard an interesting scientific explanation for what could possibly have been the cause of this devastating earthquake.

Two years before this event happened, a massive dam had been built down river from our province and the area of the quake, The Three Gorges Dam. At 7,761 feet long and with 463,000 tons of steel, it is the largest power station in the world. At full capacity, its waters rise 574 feet above sea level, 361 feet higher than the water downstream of it. On completion, it flooded 244 square miles of land. Engineers were warned at the time that this might cause too much weight on the earth in that region, but those warnings went unheeded. Now, I'm no scientist, and I'm not blaming the earthquake on the dam with all certainty, but that's a lot of water and a lot of weight! Was this natural disaster God's fault or the decision of some imperfect men who were under monetary and governmental pressure to get the task done?

The decisions of one person can have massive effect on another person (or a few million others). We see this when leaders of countries make choices that impact their entire populations. The poverty in Somalia is more related to the corruption of their government and the worldview of the people than to lack of resources. Compare it to Japan, a country who has very little natural resources yet continues to be one of the wealthiest in the world. Before we blame God, let us consider what impact we or others may have had on the circumstances at hand.

We have also been commissioned by God to tend and care for the land. We are our brother's keeper. The Bible clearly says nations will be judged by how well they cared for the poor (Matthew 25:31-46). This is not to make us feel condemned but to help us realize that we have a part to play. As humans, we are meant to help manage this earth. And as Christians, we are meant to disciple it, to bring the Kingdom of God wherever we go. How are we doing?

4) The Pain of Living in a Broken World

There was a man in Jesus' time who was blind since birth. The thinking of that era and culture was that if someone had a physical impairment it was due to some sin that either he or his ancestors had committed. So when the twelve disciples and Jesus passed by this man in John 9, they asked Jesus who it was that had caused this man's blindness, the man or his parents? Jesus responded saying, "Neither this man nor his parents sinned, but this happened so that the works of God would be displayed in him."

If that doesn't mess with your theology, I don't know what will. This happened *so that* the works of God could be seen in him?! Wow. Basically, God allowed this to happen, so that he could show his glory through this man. When Jesus spoke these words, the man was still blind...but not for long! Not with Jesus around. Jesus proceeds to tell his disciples that he is the light of the world, spits on the dirt to make mud, puts that mud on the man's eyes, and then tells him to go wash in a well-known pool. Once the man obeys, he can see. Not too shabby. This of course created a great reaction in the whole community. Everyone would have known this man as the one who had been blind since birth.

It's easy to pass over this story if we've heard it many times before, but think of a person in your circle who has a chronic disease or someone born with a physical limitation. Now imagine that person suddenly healed. What a miracle! How the goodness of God would be displayed!

After the cancerous tumor in my breast had shrunk and the doctor declared that I was "cured," I approached God with a question that had been in my heart for the entire process but about which I had been afraid to ask. Almost a year before I was diagnosed with cancer, I had attended a local meeting for moms where a speaker shared with us the importance of receiving genetic testing if cancer runs in our family. (Did I mention the cancer I had was due to a genetic mutation?)

I remember feeling quite shaken upon hearing this and reluctantly placed the little brochure that the speaker had passed out into my purse. A few days later, I made a point to take a minute to ask God if he thought this was something that I should pursue or not. I didn't hear clearly one way or another. I even had an appointment to see my gynecologist a few weeks later and broached the topic with her. She brushed it off as though it were no big deal.

So my question for God was, "Why didn't you warn me? I specifically asked you if I should get genetic testing done or not, and I didn't hear really anything in response. Why didn't you reply with a resounding, 'YES!!!' or make lightning strike or at least my hair stand on end or *something*. Why didn't you help to prevent this? Why didn't you prompt me to do the testing? It would have changed so much. Why did you remain silent?"

Before the question had even landed, I immediately felt impressed to turn to Genesis 44. I turned there and found myself in the middle of the story of Joseph. The despised younger brother turned slave, turned ruler over Egypt. As I read it, these words jumped out from the page at me:

*"'I am your brother Joseph, the one you sold into Egypt! And now, do not be distressed and do not be angry with yourselves for selling me here, because **it was to save lives that God sent me ahead of you.** For two years now there has been famine in the land, and for the next five years there will be no plowing or reaping. **But God sent me ahead of you to preserve for you a remnant on earth and to save your lives by great deliverance.'"***
Genesis 45:4-7 (emphasis mine)

And suddenly I had my answer, or at least part of it. I knew that I was meant to share my story, to help others that might be facing similar situations or giants that seemed too big to defeat. I was to point them to a God who is able to move our mountains. This is the main reason that I committed to writing this book. If I could somehow encourage someone else, then the hardship would not be in vain. But to be honest, I still felt a little cheated. I mean couldn't God have encouraged you all in some other way? Did I really have to get cancer, go through treatment, see healing come, and write a book about it for that to happen?

So the Holy Spirit graciously gave me the answer that I needed, which wasn't really an answer at all but more of an understanding that came as I was reminded of this verse:

"Not only that, but we also rejoice in our sufferings, because we know that suffering produces perseverance; perseverance, character; and character, hope. And hope does not disappoint us, because God has poured out His love into our hearts through the Holy Spirit, whom He has given us."
Romans 3:3-5

The words whispered into my heart after I had asked the million-dollar question were, *"I wanted what would come out of you after the trial."*

And with those words, I wept. I don't claim to understand it all or to know all of the answers to all of the questions, but I know that God is good. I don't believe he caused me to have cancer to teach me how to have perseverance, but he used it to do just that. I live in a broken world and was born with a broken set of genes. Just like the man born blind in Jesus' time was born with brokenness. But God received glory then and he will again. He has kept his promises to me, and I'm here to encourage you to hang onto every promise that he has and will give to you.

Chapter Four

OVERCOMING FEAR

"Fear is the path to the dark side."

Master Yoda

Calling Fear Out by Name

Fear is an emotional response. When faced with an intense emotion, I find it helpful to try to switch on the logical part of my brain. Dictionary definitions can do just that. Merriam-Webster's dictionary defines fear as "an unpleasant often strong emotion caused by anticipation or awareness of danger" or "anxious concern." I agree with you, Merriam-Webster, it's definitely unpleasant.

Some fear is natural and actually helpful. Consider the kind of fear that makes you look twice before merging into four lanes of traffic. This is a useful fear that can protect you from getting in an accident. Or the fear that keeps you from putting your hand on an open flame. This also is the protective type of fear. These are normal, everyday, dare-I-say *healthy* fears that prolong our lives, or at least their quality.

But there is a fear that is not healthy and does not help us in any way. That is the kind of fear I will be addressing in this chapter. It's the kind of fear that God does not want us to have in our lives because it can damage us, and we were not created to carry it. It comes with many aliases, from a small worry to a full-fledge panic attack. Both healthy and unhealthy fear have one purpose in common: they immobilize us. But whereas healthy fear prevents us from harm, *unhealthy* fear stops us from fully living, and that is the opposite of what God wants for us.

I like to refer to this kind of fear as "the tuck and drop." In our modest home, we have a 10-gallon aquarium with four fish and two snails (I know, it sounds like a parable.) This aquarium first started out as a small container pond in our backyard which was relocated indoors when we realized that our tiny pets might not last through a snowy winter in the great outdoors. I've been told that watching fish is meant to be calming, but these fish have not yet inspired that elusive tranquility.

They are pretty enough, I suppose, but they are extremely nervous. I suppose God found it amusing to give me four weenie fish. Actually, I think what happened is that they may have been attacked a time or two by the neighborhood squirrels or the cat that lives down the street in their outdoor days. For whatever reason, they are very skittish. Just the slightest motion from the other side of the room can send them dashing about.

The two little snails obviously move much slower, but I have noticed that whenever a fish swims frantically past them, they snails will tuck and drop. Meaning that they just tuck their feelers and sticky bodies inside of their shells and drop to the bottom of the aquarium. I don't believe they can even see or feel any movement from outside of the tank, but their instinct must tell them that if a fish goes into panic mode, danger must be near, so they tuck and drop.

I can really relate to these snails. So often, I have no logical reason to be afraid. I have no evidence that anything scary is occurring or is about to occur, yet I respond to the slightest rumor, the shortest thread on Twitter, the most grim diagnosis on WebMD, or the dimmest outlook of the nightly news, and I tuck and drop. My instincts kick in and I pull my feelers and my body inside of my shell and drop to the bottom until I discover that indeed, there was actually nothing to be afraid of. Just a dimwitted fish swimming at mach speeds for no reason. When the dust finally settles, I realize that I was taking my cues from someone who doesn't even know the truth herself.

I've been this way for as long as I can remember. In college, I elected to take a women's health course. We learned many fascinating topics about the female body, and we also learned how to give ourselves breast exams. Upon returning to my dorm room, I decided to follow the professor's illustrations and ensure that I was all clear. About halfway through my self-examination, I discovered a lump. This was the first time I had done this kind of exam on myself, but I was sure that there was an unexplained bump. So I made an appointment with a local doctor to get it checked out.

At 18 years of age, seated in a pale blue gown, sharing my discovery with the doctor, I wondered what the future might hold. She told me that she would look at it and proceeded to examine me herself. When she reached the area in which I had felt the lump, she began chuckling to herself. "Oh, honey," she smiled, "that is just your rib!" I was apparently still waiting for my "late-blooms" to appear.

This tendency played out as well during cancer treatments when I had to ban myself from googling any side effect that I was feeling or imagined that I was feeling. Because I no longer had access to top online medical information (which all somehow seemed to tell me that each symptom I had would surely lead to my imminent death), I would instead have long conversations with my doctors in which I would ask all of the questions that I no longer allowed myself to type into the search bar.

My husband, who attended these doctors visits with me, had already discovered my strange conundrums early on in marriage. I once woke him from a deep sleep in panic to tell him that my heart had stopped...let's just pause and consider what kind of person does that! Needless to say, he was prepared for these long weekly discourses between me and whichever physician or nurse that I could latch onto. He wisely downloaded some entertaining games and videos on his phone, knowing that there was no way to keep me from asking each and every curious wonder that passed through my mind over the course of the last seven days.

It got to the point that even the on-call doctor could recognize my voice due to the frequency of my calls. I kid you not. This was not some small, local, clinic. I was being seen at the largest facility in the entire state of Colorado. *And the on-call doctor knew me.* And actually, he was in fact quite comforting and helpful, assuring me that yes, I could take that supplement and no, I was most likely not having a heart attack.

The truth of the matter is that there really is so much to be afraid of in this life. It is only human to have "anxious concern" over what may be. Mixed in with the joy of life is an immense amount of pain, so we have right cause to suspect that danger might be lurking in our future. It most likely is, at some point. Like we discussed in chapter three, Jesus promised that in this world, we would have trouble. It would be naive of us to assume otherwise, even though we try to hope for the best.

Fear of this nature is often rooted in some form of unbelief which itself stems from a lie that we are believing about God's nature or character. Let me say that again because it's really important. *Fear is often rooted in a lie that we believe about God.* David Wilkerson once wrote, "Unbelief always hinders the fullness of God's revelation and blessing."[8] When we are faced with one of life's many crises, we can go down one of two paths: the path of truth and faith or the path of lies and unbelief.

For example, let's say that my car breaks down, and I don't have the money to fix it. That is a fact. I cannot wish away my car problems or pretend that they do not exist. At this moment, I have two choices that I can make. I can begin to worry about how I am going to pay for my car to get fixed or if I'll have to buy a new one all together. I can fret over how I am going to get to work without a car or how paying for this unexpected bill will deplete the funds that we've been saving up. I can explode on my kids for interrupting my train of worrisome thought and waste precious hours of sleep mulling over all of the possibilities. Choosing to entertain these what-ifs sets me on the path of fear and unbelief.

OR at that moment, I can choose the path of truth and faith. I can remind myself that God is my Shepherd and I shall not want

(Psalm 23). I will not be in need. He will provide. This is the truth, even if it doesn't feel like it at the time. God's word is truer than my emotions. As I tell myself the truth, faith begins to rise up because, as we learned in chapter two, faith comes from hearing and hearing from the word of God (Romans 10:17).

This is the same scenario that is played out in almost every trial or temptation of life. Will we choose to believe that God is good and has good plans for us, or will we choose to believe that God has rejected us and we must go at it alone? Will we choose the path of the child or that of the orphan? Orphans are abandoned and must face the world alone. Children are cared for and face their problems *with* their parents. It's the same suggestion that the serpent offered to Eve in the Garden of Eden: isn't God holding out on you? Wouldn't it be better if you took it into your own hands? And we all know how that ended.

We *will* feel fear. There's no way around it. Life is scary. And if you are wimpy like me, you may feel fear more often than others, but that does not mean that we have to be overcome by fear We have a will, and we can make choices. We do not need to be overwhelmed by life's challenges even though they do *feel* overwhelming at times. When we feel fear, we should pay attention and analyze what is at the root of that particular concern. We must ask questions: Why do I feel afraid? Is this a legitimate concern? Has God spoken to me about this in the past? What does God's Word say about this? How would God want me to respond? These questions may sound basic, but they can make a world of difference.

In 2 Corinthians 10:5, we are told to "take captive every thought and make it obedient to Christ." We must arrest each thought that comes into our minds (especially when we are feeling anxious) and cross-examine it. If the thought agrees with Jesus, it can stay. If it does not, kick it to the curb!

Sometimes I don't even realize that I am walking in fear, like when I start planning excessively. You see, I like to try to plan things out to avoid future chaos. It seems the older I get, the more I operate like this. I begin packing weeks in advance for trips and vacations. I start my Christmas shopping in August. I anticipate possible meltdowns with my children and try to have back-up plans (that often fail anyway). Now, I'm not saying it's wrong to plan, but I am saying that sometimes my planning gets a little obsessive and becomes a form of control. *If only I could plan out everything, then life can't throw me a curve ball.* Of course this is entirely untrue. And while I can save myself some stress by not procrastinating, I cannot predict every possible outcome.

This desire to control is rooted in fear and unbelief.

When life doesn't go as I planned it, I get angry or upset *because I am afraid.* I am afraid that life will begin to fall apart, in little or big ways, and I won't be able to handle it. There, I said it. That's a big lie that I have believed and still have to be careful not to fall into. This lie is rooted in the suggestion that God is not able to keep me through every storm of life, that somehow I must figure it all out by myself in order to maintain peace. Clearly, as I put this on paper, I realize how foolish it is.

There's no way that I can maintain my own peace. Sometimes I attempt the impossible, but then my son comes crashing through the front door unloading pocketfuls of collected insects from the yard all over my new rug. Or the garage door opener stops working on a day when the temperature drops below zero. Or my husband didn't fill the gas tank and I'm already running late for a meeting. You get the idea. We cannot be the source of our peace, but God can be. It *is* possible to live in a state of peace despite chaos swirling around us.

I think that must be why Jesus tells us to *consider*. In the book *A Simple Little Cure for Worry,* the author, Mark Guy Pearse points out that our minds can only focus on one thought at a time. We can either worry about what might be, or we can consider an alternative. Jesus tells us to consider the lilies because they don't fret or worry about the clothes that they are going to wear, yet they are the most beautifully clothed in all the land. Or consider the birds: they aren't consumed with fear, wondering if the crops will produce enough grain for them this year. God provides, and they receive.

We are much more important to God than the flowers of the field or the birds of the air. God will provide what we need. Besides, Jesus says that worry can't add a single hour to our lives. It literally does nothing helpful for us, but it can be the cause of a multitude of health issues. Jesus' solutions are always very simple, almost mockingly so.

Surely there has to be more to it than that, right? Just consider how God provides for sparrows and wildflowers, and we'll be at peace? But the truth is that as we logically consider how God provides for every part of creation, our thoughts are lifted up above the deafening voice of worry, and we are forced to see again that God is good and that he will provide for us, come what may. We can live not knowing what the future holds (even if it includes terrible, unsurmountable circumstances, or great, painful longing) and still be at peace.

It reminds me of a movie that I watched not too long ago, *The Prize Winner of Defiance, Ohio.* It's a true story based on the life of Evelyn Ryan, a 1950s housewife, her alcoholic husband, and their ten children (yes, ten!). Her husband cannot adequately provide for her and the kids, so she turns to competing in jingle-writing contests that are sponsored by various brands at the time. She sends in the lyrics to clever little songs or poems that she writes for whichever item that particular company is trying to sell. Over time, she proves that she is actually very good at it and wins all kind of things: sleds, boots, a pony, a car, a freezer, a shopping spree at the local grocery store, and cash money which eventually saves them from losing their home.

It's an amazing story, and Julianne Moore does a beautiful job of playing her character, but what stood out to me the most is how Evelyn consistently maintained her peace despite there being an almost constant lack in her home. At one point in the movie, after her husband has once again fumbled the ball, she turns to him and says, "I don't need you to make me happy."

Despite less than ideal circumstances for most of her adult life, she still remains in charge of her joy. She does not let worry and fear overcome her. It was actually very convicting to me. I seem to so easily let the mood of my children or husband or the guy at the grocery store change the outcome of my day. It really doesn't need to.

Now having said all of that about maintaining peace in the chaos and not allowing our emotions to dictate what the outcomes will be, I just want to clarify that I do believe that emotions are good! Emotions are gifts from God. I am not suggesting that we ignore or cut them off. They are like little

71

red flags, signaling to us what is happening inside, and we are wise to pay attention. Fear is a sign that something is wrong. It is not sinful to be afraid. It is human, and God understands this. I don't believe that is what Jesus meant when he repeatedly told his disciples to "fear not." Jesus was not referring to the *feeling* of fear, rather the *choice* to walk in that fear.

I'll never forget a picture that the Holy Spirit gave to me when I asked him how I could keep from losing my cool when my children were acting up. While I was praying about it, the image of a tea kettle on a hot stove popped into my mind. I knew instantly what it meant: tea kettles are made to whistle when they get hot. As humans, we are made to whistle when life gets to be too much. Our emotions make the noise. If I am not careful to guard my heart by taking time out for myself or saying no to needless activities on the calendar, then it is much easier for me to be stretched too thin and blow my top.

If I believe the lie that *I can't handle it* instead of the truth that I can do all things through Christ who strengthens me, I will live accordingly. If I think I can't cope, I won't. If I believe that God is in me and can give me all the wisdom, help, and provision that I need, I will keep in step with the Holy Spirit and walk in peace. Sometimes this provision comes in the form of supernatural grace and sometimes it comes in the form of a therapist. By no means do I do this perfectly, but I am at least on the journey and haven't fallen off the wagon yet.

I'm Afraid of You

At one point in my life, I was a slave to what the Bible refers to as the "fear of man." So much of what I decided to wear or say or do was based on what I thought others would think of me. I wanted to be fun and funny, to fit in and be seen as interesting. We all want that to some extent, but I had let these desires choke out the real me. I no longer was free to make choices based solely on what I wanted to do and even on what I felt *God* wanted me to do. It had become a stronghold in my life, and I needed to break free. The problem was that I couldn't. I was literally a slave to the opinions of others.

For so long I had been living like this that I didn't even realize it until the Holy Spirit began opening my eyes to the burden that I was carrying. I started to see how much impact the comments of friends and strangers had on my choices and decisions. I was an approval addict. I realized that I wanted to be free. That is the first step in breaking away from fear: wanting liberation. The second step is believing that freedom is possible.

As God unveiled these truths to me, there were practical steps that I knew I needed to take along the way. Faith leads to action. I sensed the Holy Spirit was nudging me to do random acts of boldness that would help dislodge this thorn of fear. Sometimes they were little steps of obedience like, "Don't wear any make-up today," (I was in my 20s, so this wasn't as scary as it would be now!) or, "Spend more time this week reading in the Bible about my thoughts and feelings towards you," or, "Stop reading women's magazines for awhile to detox yourself." Other times, they felt more confronting like, "Ask the cashier if she would like prayer for anything." I was petrified that God would ask me to do something that I would not be able to, but he never did.

God wants us to pass all of the tests that we are given. Although I sometimes ignored the nudges and wonder what stories I would have if I would have followed, many times I listened and obeyed. Slowly but surely, the fear of man began to loosen its grip. These nudges are not rules that everyone should follow if they want to get free from fear of man. Everyone must listen and keep in step with the Spirit in their own lives. I share them only to show that God may ask you to take part in your own breakthrough. The power is from him but we must surrender to his wisdom and leading if we want to see his results.

Getting free from the need to have everyone's approval is a much different kind of fear than the thought of losing a loved one or facing a life-threatening illness, but learning how to walk out steps of faith in those seasons helped to prepare me for battles ahead. And although approval addiction might seem small in light of other, larger disasters, the impact of it on one's life can be profound. Just as David was prepared to fight Goliath by defending his sheep from bears and lions, so are we prepared for what our futures hold.

Buying Baby Rattles Under Siege

I was recently sorting through some old items that I had stored away in a box and came across an old baby rattle. It was one my son played with when he was just a teeny, bitty thing. It's worn now with nicks and teeth marks. To anyone else, it is just a cheap rattle, but to me it represents a physical act of faith. A reminder of the Lord's covenant to me.

Like most young married couples with hopes of starting a family, my husband and I were so excited when the day came that we saw that first positive pregnancy test! We were living in East Asia at the time, so baby clothes and cards of congratulations from family around the globe began pouring in after our big announcement. As a responsible new mom, I began eating healthier and trying to get more rest. I spent my days dreaming of and praying over what this child would become. We went through lists of potential names and ideas of how to decorate a nursery. I even remember asking the Lord randomly as I was lying in bed one night what the name of this child should be. Not really expecting an answer, the name Joseph popped into my head. "Hmmm...nah," I responded and drifted off to sleep.

The prophet Jeremiah had his own baby rattle of sorts as well. In Jeremiah 32, we read that the Babylonian army has moved onto the land of Israel and placed it under siege. Israel is about to be overtaken by her enemies. In fact, God tell them, "You ARE going to be overtaken by your enemies." The situation is dismal. It's a war zone, and it's only going to get worse. They are suffering huge losses. Lack of food and healthcare, family members and friends dying. They are about to become refugees and lose everything. I can't think of too many situations worse than what the Israelites were experiencing at that moment. And yet, in the midst of all of this heartbreak, God tells Jeremiah, the prophet to go and buy a field.

Say what, God?! The land is torn apart, the entire area covered in famine, and the city at the edge of invasion, yet God speaks to Jeremiah and asks him to purchase a field, to invest his money and his heart in this seemingly forsaken land. It would be like purchasing your retirement acreage in an area controlled by ISIS. But God promises Jeremiah that one day this land will again see weddings and dances, joy and singing. So, with no physical evidence that there is any possible way that what God is saying could actually come to pass, Jeremiah does as the Lord says, and purchases the property. Years later, God restores the land of Israel and Jeremiah's field is redeemed, but at the time, all that Jeremiah had to hold onto was God's promise.

Shortly after the initial stage of my early pregnancy bliss, complications began. I started spotting, so I went to the doctor and was told to take it easy. I tried to stay off my feet more, but the bleeding increased. By the time we hit the 3-month mark, the situation did not look good. We went in to get an ultrasound and no heartbeat was found.

The tiny baby had stopped growing and was no longer with us. Our first child had left us for Heaven. I didn't want to let go and apparently, neither did my body. I was told that I should have fully miscarried by now, but for some reason, my body was not responding. So I would need surgery to remove the remains of my tiny child and any other tissue. We were devastated. We flew to Hong Kong where the facilities were better and surgery would be safer. I remember the heavy blanket of sadness that covered me the morning after when I awoke and realized that my child was no longer inside of the womb that was meant to protect him.

We were told by our doctor there to wait a year before trying again. So for the next year, I grieved what we had lost. When the year came to an end, with high hopes and strained optimism, we did try again. This time, I got pregnant very quickly...but I also miscarried very quickly. Two babies. Two scars. Two big question marks for God.

I remember laying face down on the rug one day in our small high-rise apartment and sobbing. I wept for what we'd lost. I wept for what may never be. Hope was nowhere to be found. I was petrified to try again. I was too sad and tired and scared to fight or worship or even open the Bible. I was just pouring out my heart to God, wondering how to move forward and if biological children were even in our future. I was petrified to take the next step and trying to come to terms with all of it when I was reminded of the name that I had received before I knew our tiny baby had died: Joseph. What did Joseph mean? I knew his story from the Bible, so I did a little research and found that there were two Hebrew meanings within the name: *"taken away"* and *"may he add another."* My jaw dropped.

As I read the truth of the name that the Holy Spirit had preemptively placed in my heart, I wept. Yes, our first baby, Joseph, was taken away, but *God would add another.* This one name summed up exactly the space that I found myself in. That in-between world of having a child taken away yet longing for another to be added.

So we began to hope for another. I was still terrified after losing two, but we visited with doctors and received advice and prayed. And eventually, a third pregnancy was confirmed. Initial excitement was followed by intense fear. All the what-if questions came at me like a flood. I would wake up in the middle of the night, horrified that I was bleeding or had already lost the baby again. I prayed for life. Rich and I prayed for life. We recruited all of our friends and family to pray for life. I hung up Scriptures that I felt God had given to encourage me all over the room. And then...I started spotting again. I was undone. I literally did not know how to move even one step ahead. I cried out to God. It was all I could do.

And God told me, as he told Jeremiah, to go and buy a field. In the midst of what looked hopeless, with fear pressing in and the potential of death literally just around the corner, I was told to go and buy a field. I could not shake this Holy Spirit thought. I felt that I was meant to step out with whatever faith I could muster and take some sort of action. God was extending his hand to me and saying, "Do you trust me?" I somehow knew I was meant to buy something that this pre-born baby would one day play with as an act of faith.

At first, I ignored the thought. I didn't want to be foolish and fix my faith on my own imaginations. But the thought persisted. I didn't want to say it aloud and admit that God might be asking me to take a position of faith in something that would break me if it didn't work out. For days I resisted this nudging until I came across a verse in Isaiah 49:

The children you shall have, after you have lost the others, shall say again in your ears: this place is too narrow for me.
Give me a place that I might dwell.

I told Rich what I felt like God was impressing upon my heart. He agreed it was right, so we went to the store. We searched until we found a small set of plastic baby rattles that we could afford. We paid for them and brought them home, and I set them up as a reminder of what God had spoken.

Even though there was more spotting, I continued to cling to the promises that the Holy Spirit was whispering to me. Promises of life and hope. With every one, I was still petrified. I never felt "full of faith," but I learned in the process that faith is not reliant on our emotions. Faith is a choice to believe God, even when we can barely breathe. Somedays, it felt like I battled thoughts of doubt every minute. It was really hard work to continue to come back each time to the truth that God is good, and he does not lie.

And God proved himself faithful. After nine months, a very healthy (and huge) 10 pound, 12 ounce baby boy was born to us. I recalled God's faithfulness every time he shook that little rattle in his hands. And all those prayers that I prayed for him to have a strong will to live while he was in the womb were answered. This boy is determined to live. I see it everyday in his sense of wonder and strong, persistent will. We gave him the name Benjamin, the son that was added after his older brother Joseph, just like in the Bible. God answered my prayer, but more than that, actually. God was the one who first put the hope in my heart, drew me to pray for it, and then fulfilled the seed that he himself had planted.

The Antidote to Fear

In 1 John 4:18, we read that *"perfect love drives out fear."* Fear cannot remain in the presence of perfect love, God's perfect love. *We* will never be perfect or have perfect love, but *he* already loves us perfectly. The more that we come to realize this truth, the less fear will have a grip on our lives. God's love is light and fear is darkness. When the light switch is flipped on, darkness is squeezed out.

There's been times in my life where the fear has been so strong, it's felt like a physical wave descending upon me. The only relief that I can find in those times of intense fear is to turn to worship. I go into my room, close the door, and put on songs that lift God up. In song, I recite the truth of his Word and remind myself of his character, his faithfulness, his power, his love. I sing them to my own soul. I sing them out in defiance of the darkness. I take my eyes off my towering Goliaths and get them onto the Creator of the universe, and when I do, the giants no longer seem so big.

My mother had cancer back in the 80s. I was only four and my brother was two. By the time they diagnosed her, it had already spread throughout her whole body. The doctors said her chance of survival was slim, but she had a strong sense that God was going to heal her. In those days, cancer treatment was extreme with little to no help for the side effects. She was told if she did survive the cancer, the side effects from the chemotherapy and radiation would likely kill her within the next five years.

There were days when she could not leave the hospital because of the treatment's impact. No one was allowed into her room for 48 hours after radiation. Even the nurses had to give her food by slipping their hands through holes in the wall due to the fear that it could harm them as well.

At night, she said the fear of dying was the strongest. It was almost as she could feel it trying to invade her room. She remembers being tempted to plan out her own funeral in her mind: which dress she would wear, the music that would be played, the kinds of flowers to be ordered. The only relief she found was by playing cassette tapes that were filled with God's Word and the testimonies of what he had done for others. She would listen to them on repeat until she fell asleep or morning came. She kept choosing life in the face of death. She taught me that you can choose to agree with fear or you can use God's word against it. And she was healed of that cancer 35 years ago.

This is exactly what we see Jesus do when he is tempted by Satan in the desert. Three times, the devil comes at him tempting him to disobey the Father. Satan promises fame and power in return for bowing down to him. But all three times, Jesus counters him with "it is written." When the enemy comes in like a flood, God's word is the standard that protects us. And Jesus is the Word of God. God will lead us out of fear's temptation and into freedom, step by step. There will be grace for each step that we must walk *as we get to that step*. There is generally little grace for the steps up ahead because we are not there yet. But there is grace for the step that we are on right now.

Jesus speaks of this grace when he tells his disciples not to worry about what they will say when they are brought before rulers and authorities to be questioned. He promised them that the Holy Spirit would teach them just what to do in their moment of need (Luke 12:11-12).

Once while living in East Asia, Rich and I and two friends were taken into custody by the police because I had given a Christian tract to a local woman and was spotted by a plainclothes policeman. Less than three percent of our city of nine million people were Christian, and most had never heard about Jesus. This particular woman who received the tract had never even considered God before, but she wanted to learn more.

We were due to catch a bus so after chatting with her for a while, I left her with a small booklet that explained more. We had handed out tracts many times before with no consequence, but for whatever reason, on that particular day the authorities were notified. Within just a few minutes, a police van pulled up to the scene and we were told to climb inside.

It was the strangest sensation. All four of us crouched inside the little van and began silently praying. About halfway into town, for no apparent reason, the van pulled to the side of the road and we were ordered out. We were confused but relieved. After we found our own way back into the city, we discovered that another pair of state officials were waiting for us. It was then that we were questioned about the nature and origin of the Christian pamphlets.

Since I was the one that had actually given the woman the tract, they questioned me the most. Although I had never experienced anything like this before, I knew just how to answer them. I took the role of a naive foreigner and responded with my own questions, "Oh, you can't do that here?" and, "Is that not allowed?" "Thank you for informing me." After a mild interrogation, we were instructed not to do anything of the sort again, and then they left. God gave me the words that I needed at just the right time.

Corrie Ten Boom also writes of this timely grace in her book *The Hiding Place.* Corrie was a young Dutch woman who secretly housed Jewish people in her family home during the Second World War. She was eventually discovered and sent to a concentration camp. She tells of a time as a child when she was worried about her parents dying. She was afraid that she would never be able to bear the pain of that loss. This is how her discerning father responded to her:

"Father sat down on the edge of the narrow bed. 'Corrie,' he began gently, 'when you and I go to Amsterdam- when do I give you your ticket?'
I sniffed a few time, considering this.
'Why, just before we get on the train.'
'Exactly. And our wise Father in heaven knows when we're going to need things, too. Don't run out ahead of Him, Corrie.

When the time comes that some of us will have to die, you will look into your heart and find the strength you need- just in time.'"

How often the words of Corrie's father came to mind as I received my own cancer diagnosis and began to look ahead to all of the treatments that would be required. Grace was provided for each step *as it was needed.* I tried often to follow Jesus' kind advice and not worry about tomorrow because tomorrow will bring its own worries. We literally only have *this* moment to live. It is the only one we are guaranteed. The others must be left up to him.

Feeling Fearless

You know in the movies when the guy who has lost everything is no longer afraid of anything? He no longer has anything left to lose, so fear has nothing that it can latch onto. There is no longer anything left in his life that can hold him back from doing that last heroic deed. I believe there is a way that we can find and live in this type of freedom as well.

In the Bible, Jesus speaks of slaves and sons. Slaves are afraid. They live in constant fear of punishment, wondering what might be done to them or taken from them. But sons live as rightful heirs, knowing that they have a loving Father who will help them with whatever comes. The path of surrender is the path of sonship. If I can place life's most precious possessions in the hands of a loving God and surrender them to his care and guidance, then I am free from the burden of trying to protect them myself. And honestly, I can't even do it well anyway.

We are slaves to that which we determine we cannot live without. One of the largest speed bumps I encountered on the road to pursuing a calling in full time missions was the fear that I would never marry. I doubted how I would ever find a suitable husband if I gave myself fully to a career that seemed to be stuffed full of single women. I felt challenged by the Holy Spirit to lay down my "right" to be married. It was not that he said I would never wed, but I was holding so tightly to this desire that it was getting in the way of what he wanted to give me.

After much wrestling and many tears, I was able to lay this hope at the Lord's feet. I chose to trust that if marriage was his best for me, he could find me a husband even in the middle of Timbuktu. And if he had other plans, I would trust him with those as well. I came to the point where I was willing to agree with him that I did not need a spouse to make me whole. I was already whole in Jesus. Once I gave up what I thought I could not live without, I was free.

Before I lost my mother, to her second bout of cancer in 2013, the thought of living without her was devastating. It still is, in fact, but God gave my family the grace to walk through each step of that season, and he continues to do so. My greatest fear now is the threat that I will lose those that I love or that we will experience unsustainable hardship and pain. If I can somehow manage to name this fear and entrust my most precious people over to God and his care, I can find freedom. This is surrender.

I wonder also if it is not the greatest act of faith, entrusting our loved ones to God, just as he entrusted his only Son to us. It is part of the daily call to lay down our lives before him, and we are told if we want to find our lives then we must give them up.

When I lost my hair during chemotherapy, I noticed a strange transformation take place. After it all fell out, I began to wear head coverings. There were many interesting side effects that happened during cancer treatment but the most surprising one of all came with the wearing of these "chemo caps."

Some were scarves, some were cotton night caps for sleeping, some were stylish turbans, but they all had one thing in common: whenever I put them on in public, I was totally fearless. I was untouchable. I mean, who's gonna mess with a woman battling cancer? People parted before me and went out of their way to help me. Scenarios that would have inspired fear in the past now only invoked a mere smirk.

I remember walking down the streets of a rougher area in Denver one day, passing some shady looking young men (maybe they were gangsters, who knows?). In the past, I might have crossed the street or clutched my purse a little tighter. At the least, I would have avoided eye contact, but this time, I did neither. I had my chemo cap on, and I was not going to be messed with. I kept my pace up, strong and proud, and brashly looked directly in their eyes as we passed. They were the ones who looked away and allowed room for me on the sidewalk! It was amazing! The chemo cap had some miraculous power to make me feel invincible. I wasn't afraid of anyone!

I suppose I became a little drunk on its power and began to use it in other inappropriate places as well. Richard eventually suggested that I needed to reign it in. I couldn't continue on in this fashion: threatening the kid who tripped my son during a soccer game or stealing people's parkings spots, at least not with him in the car. I may have the chemo cap on, but my husband could still reap some unpleasant repercussions if I pushed the limits too far.

Now that my hair has grown out, I remember the power of the chemo caps with longing. Don't get me wrong, I was totally ready to get rid of those things, but what was it about the hats gave me that awesome sauce? Perhaps it was the same effect that those guys in the movies with nothing to lose experienced. I was already looking death in the face. What else was there to be afraid of? Fine, steal my purse, beat me up, tell me my kid got sent to the principal's office. I'm made of steel. Suddenly all the small worries of life seemed like no big deal. They rolled off like water off a duck's back. It was the power of having nothing to lose, the power of a surrendered life. This is where freedom lives.

I confess, I don't live each day like that anymore. But I do often remember how unimportant most of life's stresses are. And I often ask myself, "What are you so afraid of?" What's the worst that could happen? The bill isn't paid on time and you have no electricity for a day until you go down to the office and pay it? Your child sasses her friends and has to learn the hard way what happens when you hurt people's feelings? You leave your clothes in the dryer for three days and have to rewash them because of the wrinkles? You lose your job and have to trust God to provide in a new way?

What are you so afraid of? Isn't God big enough, loving enough, powerful enough to handle it? If my answer is no, then I am harboring an idol. I'm trusting in something or someone else more than I am trusting in God. And idolatry produces fear. If I think that money or a spouse or children or friends or a perfect complexion will fulfill my every need and desire then I will be sadly disappointed. To find freedom, I must lay down my rights to these gifts or they will become burdens. It's not until everything in my life is surrendered to the Creator that fear loses its grip. No more sting, no more threat. A surrendered life is one of peace. And that my friends, is the opposite of fear.

Chapter Five

OBTAINING YOUR INHERITANCE

"It's not what you look at that matters, it's what you see."

Henry David Thoreau

You're Already Free

The Emancipation Proclamation was an executive order issued by President Abraham Lincoln that went into effect in 1863. Because of this new law, the status of 3.5 million slaves in America changed overnight from slave to that of a free person. This was indeed life-changing news! The announcement didn't trickle down to all areas though, so some slaves, especially those in areas more removed from the Civil War battles, did not know this law had been passed. It wasn't until June 19, 1865 that this proclamation was announced and enforced in more remote areas, particularly in Texas. So for nearly two and a half years, many free men and women were still functioning as slaves.

Many Christians still live in spiritual slavery today. When Jesus died and was resurrected over 2,000 years ago, he bought us freedom from slavery. It was God's great Emancipation Proclamation to the world. No longer do we need to live as slaves to sin and to our own evil desires. No longer do we need to live under the curse of sickness and death. Jesus took that curse upon himself (Galatians 3:13).

God has provided all that we need to walk in freedom and wholeness: spiritually, mentally, and physically. What many of us lack is the knowledge and understanding that he has already given us all that we need. Here are some great verses to prove this point (emphases are mine):

*"Praise be to the God and Father of our Lord Jesus Christ! In his great mercy he has given us **new birth** into a living hope through the resurrection of Jesus Christ from the dead."*
1 Peter 1:3

*"Praise be to the God and Father of our Lord Jesus Christ, who has blessed us in the heavenly realms with **every spiritual blessing** in Christ."*
Ephesians 1:3

*"'He himself bore our sins' in his body on the cross, **so that we might die to sins and live for righteousness**; 'by his wounds you have been healed.'"*
1 Peter 2:24

The Lord has *already provided* joy and peace and patience and all the fruits of righteousness in the Holy Spirit. If we have given our lives to him, we are one with him. We merely need to keep in step with his leading. We no longer need to come under hopelessness and discouragement, fear and anxiety. I believe sickness is also included in this promise. In Matthew 8:17, it tells us that Jesus "took up our infirmities and bore our diseases." Everyone who came to Jesus and asked for healing in the Gospels was healed! Every. Single. Person. Have I seen every sick person that I prayed for get healed? No, but that doesn't negate the fact that Jesus did. As I mentioned before, every day around the world, people see supernatural healings and provision.

If you read through the New Testament, you will notice that the authors write from a place of us having *already received* everything they need in Jesus. The problem is not that we don't have it. The problem is that we don't *believe* that we have it. This understanding changes everything. No longer are we begging God for help when we pray, twisting his arm to do what we want. *We are no longer servants but sons* (Galatians 4:7). That means that we have already inherited what is our Father's. He's already given us everything. He's already done what's needed. It's a finished work. We just need to live and pray in agreement with him and according to his will. He is the initiator; we respond to his leading. The prayers themselves may sound the same, but the motivation has changed. This change in perspective is huge.

Let's imagine that when you turned 16 your parents came to you and handed over the keys to a new car. They bought the car, and the title is in their names, but they are giving it to you. You have the keys. You have the authority to drive this car. Awesome! I would have been super excited. When I turned 16, I got our old 1984 family Jeep, and I was still pretty happy about that. When I received the keys for the Jeep, I went out to the driveway, put them in the ignition, and excitedly drove into town.

But what if we choose *not* to believe that our parents had really given us the keys to this car. What if we didn't believe it was ours or didn't think they keys would work? What if we were too scared to drive? Well, then we wouldn't have the benefit of all that a car can provide. Would our parents love us less? No, but we wouldn't be experiencing the fullness of the blessing that they were trying to give.

It's the same way for us now with the promises of God. We can't see the promises like we can see a new car, but we must believe that they are real and that they are *ours* if we are going to access them. The Bible says in Hebrews 11:6, "And without faith it is impossible to please God, because anyone who comes to him must believe that he exists and that he rewards those who earnestly seek him."

Faith precedes the actualization of the promise.

Step one: God gives a promise, a proclamation of what will come. *Step two:* we believe that what he said is true. *Step three:* we begin to live in agreement with his truth and see the promise actualized. This is not just positive thinking or manifesting your own reality. And this is not just a "name it and claim it" scenario. Our faith needs to be based on what God says and not merely on what we would like to see happen. Let's go back to God's Word to see this more clearly illustrated.

One of the most powerful examples of this happening is in the book of Numbers. God made a promise to the Israelites that he has already reserved a Promised Land for them. They had been slaves in Egypt for over 400 years when God broke through and rescued them out of bondage. He led them through the desert and onto the brink of a land flowing with milk and honey.

Everything they could have ever imagined was there. Total provision and protection. God wills this land to them. The only problem is that the land was already occupied by a brutal and warlike people, the Canaanites. They were huge, literally, and they were ruthless. So there's this dichotomy at play for the Israelites. The land is theirs, but they have to take it by force. The land has already been given to them by God, and he promised that they *will* defeat their enemies. But they have to fight for it.

Moses, who is the leader of the Israelites at the time, sends out twelve spies into this land. He tells them to bring back a report of all that they see. Upon returning, they all agree that, yes, this land is very good. It indeed flows with milk and honey, and the grapes are so big that it took two men to carry one bunch back to show the others. But the big catch is that the people who inhabit this land are terrifying. Ten of the spies do not want to try to inhabit the land. Only two of the spies, Joshua and Caleb believe that they can actually make the land their own.

All twelves spies observed the same land and the same giants, but only two of them believed that God would help him like he said he would. Joshua and Caleb tried to encourage the people to not be afraid, but the voice of the other ten was louder. It invoked great fear throughout the entire camp until the rest of the Israelites agreed with their fearful report and decided that they dared not enter the land.

All of the spies saw the same beautiful land covered with bountiful crops, but only two of the spies were totally confident that they could take on the colossal enemies who also resided in the land. So what was the difference? They saw the exact same landscape and went on the same journey, so why did ten come back defeated and two come back encouraged? Personality differences? Fake news? No. The only difference was their *perspective*. Ten saw through their own natural eyes while the other two saw through the eyes of God's promises.

I can't imagine what those spies were feeling when the saw such a terrifying opponent living in the land that had been promised to them, but I do know what it feels like to be up against an adversary that wants to take your life. An aggressive one that will stop at nothing to consume you and wants to destroy all that you have. God told me that he was going to heal me from cancer, but that did not mean that the journey was going to be easy. I had a choice in how I wanted to proceed. It was not reliant on my strength or ability, but I did need to agree with what God had said.

Faith Beyond the Outcome

I also want to make it very clear that those who do not experience healing are certainly not in any way less than those who do. An undesirable outcome is not necessarily due to a lack of faith. A former missionary once shared with me how she spent hours at her stepfather's hospital bedside, praying for healing. She completely believed that he would be healed. She had witnessed God miraculously heal in the past, and she was confident he would do it again. She imagined her stepdad arising from the bed and going home with her. Her faith did not wane, but her prayer was not answered like she hoped. Her stepfather passed despite the faith that she had.

My personal battle was cancer. If I would have had to trust to receive healing for paralysis or a chronic illness, would I have had the courage to step out on that promise? I can't say. No one can fully know what goes on between an individual and God when they are looking sickness or death in the face. No one can fully imagine what transpires there. This is again why I believe it's so important to seek God's face *personally* in every situation that we face and stand on the word that he gives us. There may come a time when God says to let go and stop praying for healing. He will make the next step clear to us as we walk with him.

I've wondered many times why my mom was not healed when she knew and believed in God's promises. I also realize that there is a time and place for each person to leave this earth, and this is not always the time and place that we, as finite creatures, want. There is also weariness that enters when the battle is long. Sometimes healing is delayed and the wait between the promise and the provision is extremely difficult. There are many who ask God to free them from the agony of it all, and I don't blame them *one bit!* There is absolutely no judgement on my part if you throw in the towel and ask God to take you home.

During my mother's final days on earth, as the cancer stole all of the remaining life and health from her body and mind, and she became a shell of the woman that she once was, we began to ask God to take her Home. Could we still have seen a healing if we would have prayed in faith for it? Yes, I think so, but we were so devastated, and it was so painful to watch her that we just asked for mercy.

It's so hard to make decisions when you are the one on the battlefield. It's so easy to stand from afar and know exactly what should have been done. Think of all the parenting advice I had before I actually became a parent! But even if we miss it, we still win. Because of what Jesus did for us, I can confidently say that I will be with my mother again one day. No, we did not see her healing take place on earth. It's possible she may have been healed had we stood in greater faith. That's just the reality of life.

I don't feel condemned if someone tells me that I didn't have enough faith. It's very possible that I didn't. I know that. It would have been hurtful if someone would have told me this shortly after she passed, but looking back now, I can see it all more clearly. Even in my lack, God still came through. Because of Jesus, I can still sing out the words of 1 Corinthians 15:55, "Where, O death is your victory? Where, O death, is your sting?" Even in our deficiency, his sufficient sacrifice has made wholeness possible.

Following Jesus doesn't mean all sunshine. Surrendering our lives to him means that we choose to trust that he is good and will do what is best for us, even if it's not what we want. We see this when Jesus faces the prospective cross. In Matthew 16, Jesus is trying to tell his disciples what is going to happen to him, to somehow prepare them for what will come. At this point, Peter actually rebukes Jesus! Can you imagine? Rebuking God. "Heaven forbid!" he says, "This will never happen to you!" Sometimes I hear preachers talk like Peter, telling us that bad outcomes should never happen to us, that we should always expect the pot of gold at the end of the rainbow.

But Jesus shut down Peter's rant and called him out. He told Peter that he was not seeing from God's point of view but man's. He actually called Peter *Satan*, so that's one way to quiet down your opponents. Jesus said that this kind of response to his upcoming trial was a dangerous trap to him. Why? Because it's such a temptation to want everything to be easy and go well. Who wants to walk through pain? We were not made for it. We were not created for death and devastation, but here we are, living outside of Eden.

We see this situation again with Paul, when he is headed to Jerusalem. Someone in one of the churches gets a word of knowledge from God that "chains await him there," but Paul already knows this. The church doesn't want him to go for fear of what will happen to him, but Paul goes willingly because he feels called to share the gospel in Rome after visiting Jerusalem.

I do not propose that life will always be easy and nothing bad should ever happen to you, but it's not God's intention that we stay in the valley of the shadow of death forever. At the end of that psalm (Psalm 23), the shepherd brings his sheep out to a beautifully prepared meadow where they find provision and safety. Like Winston Churchill said, "If you're going through hell, keep going." Have hope that healing and wholeness is available to you as you walk through the valley with your Shepherd. Even if you are called to the cross, the cross was not the end. The resurrection was. God's ultimate plan will end in your good and in your wholeness. Even if you lose, you win because of what Jesus did for you.

When to Press On and When to Let Go

How do we know when we are to stand and fight for healing and when we are to let go? There has to be a personal confirmation in your spirit, initiated by God, but I believe that *in general*, God wants to heal. It's who he is. He is a healer. Unless he has made it clear to me that he intends for something other than healing, that this cross is what he's allowing for some reason, then I pray for healing because that is what I see modeled in Jesus. Jesus is the image of the invisible God. Whatever we think we know about God must be measured against the plumbline that is Jesus Christ. Whatever Jesus does and says is what God does and says. No exceptions. And Jesus always healed. Jesus didn't heal *everyone*, but he always healed everyone who asked him.

Jesus told his disciples to heal the sick, cleanse the lepers, and drive out demons, because that is God's ultimate purpose for us: healing, cleansing, and freedom from demonic oppression. Jesus was ten for ten in his ability to do this. The disciples were not. We are not. We are going to miss it. There will be times when we do not see the breakthrough that we are asking for. I don't know all of the reasons why, but we must be careful not to pull back in fear and hide under the covers of "safe" theology just because we experience failure and feel embarrassed or disappointed.

My hope is that you will hear the message throughout this book that God wants to bring you breakthrough. But I also hope that you hear that if breakthrough doesn't happen or if you fail or miss it, there's absolutely no condemnation in it at all. I have missed it so many times on my multiple trapeze acts of faith, but I've always dropped into a net of grace. Never once has he allowed me to hit the ground.

In the case of the Israelites and the twelve spies, they chose to believe the witness of the ten who were afraid. The Israelites did not believe God and because of this, they missed out on their Promised Land. God allowed that generation to miss out on what he had prepared for them and waited until the next generation was ready to take the land. Did God want them to be excluded from his promises? Not at all. He was offering it fully to them. It was their own choice to mistrust God that held them back from all that he had prepared for them. They *would not* believe in God's promise. In Deuteronomy 14:11, God says, "they *refuse* to believe in me," and Psalm 106:24 says, "They *refused* to enter the Promised Land, for they *would not* believe his solemn oath to care for them." This is more than "I believe, help my unbelief." This is an outright determination to turn back in fear instead of making a choice to believe that God can do what he says he can do.

Jesus experienced this kind of refusal to believe in God as well. In John 12:37, we read, "Even after Jesus had performed so many signs in their presence, they still would not believe in him." Just because we have seen God move does not mean that we will automatically believe him every time he speaks. We have the same choice that the twelve spies and the people in Jesus' time did. The weight of that truth can feel scary because it doesn't always make sense. Sometimes we will miss it, but that does not negate the fact that what God says is true. This is just how it works: to see the promises of God actualize in our lives and the world around us, we must believe him and step out in faith. How else can it function? James 2:20 confirms it, "Faith without works is dead." The relieving news in all of this is that we truly only need a mustard seed of faith to be able to take the next step.

Faith increases as we exercise it.

If I tell my child that I have a bathtub full of chocolates waiting for him, but he chooses to not believe me and never peeks in the bathroom to check it out, what more can I do? It's his choice. I can try to convince him. I can remind him of all the other times that I have promised him something and it came to pass, but I can't make him enter into the bathtub of chocolates if he doesn't want to go. Unless I do it by force. And God isn't a bully. He doesn't lead us by force, rather he gives us a choice and a free will to decide what we want to do. Sometimes I wish he wouldn't, but then we would just be robots.

If you are part of a denomination or belief system that does not include healings and miracles, I would encourage you to go through the Bible yourself and decide what is true. Research it. Seek out other people who have experienced miracles. Go as far as visiting the places where the miracles are occurring. Why not? Faith doesn't need to be blind. In John 10:38, Jesus himself said, "Even though you do not believe in me, believe the works themselves." I have seen people who do not even know God experience healing and come to believe in him that way. The works (the miracles) are the evidence that God is real and he cares about them.

That's the point. God cares about us. He cares about you. In Matthew 7:9, Jesus says, "Which of you, if your child asks for bread will give him a stone? Or if he asks for a fish, will give him a snake? So if you who are evil know how to give good gifts to your children, how much more will your Father in heaven give good things to those who ask him!" God wants to give us good gifts, but there are times that we must remain faithful in between the promise and the realization of that promise.

"When the Son of Man returns, how many will he find on the earth who have faith."
Luke 18:8

Faith is the open door that allows God to enter.

God is continually drawing us into greater levels of knowing and trusting him. Faith does not mean you have to pretend as if everything is fine when it isn't. Faith isn't ignoring reality, but neither is it letting reality determine what is truth. What is real does not always equal what is *true*. When God told me that he would heal me, I still had cancer in my body. When he said that I was going to have a child, I still miscarried. And when he said he would provide for me, not all the money was yet in the bank.

There is often space between what God says and the time when he brings it to pass, and this space must be filled with our faith. Of course, God can make it happen even if we don't believe, but in general, those that believe are the ones who receive what he promises.

We understand this concept when it comes to our salvation. We believe *by faith* that Jesus died on the cross and rose again. We believe that through this eternal plan, the forgiveness of sins is offered to the entire world. Anyone who wants it can have the keys to the eternal life. It's there for everyone, but not everyone accesses it by faith

Practically, this can take many shapes. For example, it can simply mean standing on God's word when bad reports come. It might mean choosing to walk in confidence that God will provide after job loss instead of being fearful that there won't be enough. It may mean making decisions based on what God has said instead of what we think or feel. It can mean asking God how much to give to a person in need instead of asking our bank accounts, trusting in faith that God will provide for our own needs.

When my mother was diagnosed with cancer the first time in 1984, she felt strongly that God said he would bring a good report. But for the next few months, all she heard were bad reports. Reports that said the cancer had spread all over her body. Reports that said the treatment would most likely not work. And reports that gave her an eighty percent chance of dying. But she chose to believe the truth of God's promise over her present reality.

She prayed prayers like this: *"Thank you, God that you have paid the price for my healing. By your stripes, I am healed. I curse this cancer and command it to go. Thank you that the Spirit of him who raised Jesus from the dead is living in me, and he who raised Christ from the dead will also give life to my mortal body because of your Spirit who lives within me (Romans 8:11). I agree that I have God's Spirit in me and he is giving life to my body."* It took many months and much trusting, but her good report finally came. If you have a promise from God, don't let go of it until he brings it to pass.

When You Still Need a Fleece

I find the story of Gideon to be very encouraging because Gideon was a total weenie. We find him first in Judges 6 when enemies had overtaken the land that once belonged to his forefathers and the Israelites were living in constant fear. The night that God intervened in Gideon's life, he was hiding out in a winepress, threshing his wheat there so that no one would find him. An angel of the Lord came to him and called him a "mighty warrior". I can just imagine Gideon's face. Here he is, fearing for his life yet being told that in fact, he is a great warrior. I wonder if he looked around to make sure the angel was speaking to him. *You talkin' to me?* Gideon actually goes so far as to question the angel as to why God hasn't rescued his people yet if he cares so much about them.

The angel goes on to tell Gideon that God is indeed going to rescue his people. In fact, he is going to use Gideon to accomplish that task. Gideon questions how this is going to happen since his clan is the weakest in all of Israel, and he is the wimpiest one in his clan! God responds by simply telling Gideon that he will be with him. When Gideon asks for a sign as confirmation, God gives him one.

I love that even though Gideon was indeed a super wimp when God first called him, God didn't let Gideon's *reality* trump the *truth* that he was made to be a man of courage. Gideon could have run away and ignored what God was saying, but he chose to stay and step out into a new reality, and now his story is in the Bible. Step by feeble step, he began to live out the destiny that the angel spoke over his life. He required a bunch of signs and encouragement from the Lord along the way (a bit of a high-maintenance hero), but God gave him what he asked for and eventually the enemy was routed at the hand of the mighty warrior otherwise known as Gideon.

This story gives me so much hope. We too may be hiding out, camped out under the shadow of our own reality, but God is calling us to step out of the shadow and into our destinies. If we heed his whispers telling us who we really are, we can find the courage to begin. We already possess all that we need for the journey. We just need to believe it. When we reach the end of our stories, we will be able to look back and see all of the good that God has brought about in and through us.

Chapter Six

THE IMPORTANCE OF COMMUNITY

"I love mankind...it's people I can't stand!"

Linus

Not Good to Be Alone

When God made Adam, I wonder if he waited a while to create Eve, just to give Adam a chance to realize that he was missing something. Surely, God would have known that he was going to be creating another human, a woman to represent the other half of his image. She would help Adam care for the Garden and start a family. Why did God wait to make Eve? Whatever the reason, God made it clear in Genesis 2:18 that it is not good for man to be alone. We were made to live in community, and we require it if we want to live our best lives.

A few years back, Cigna conducted a survey on 20,000 adults over 18 years old.[9] They found that nearly half (46%) of Americans feel alone. Loneliness rates have doubled in the last few decades, and our young people are feeling the brunt of it. Former U.S. Surgeon General, Vivek H Murthy called it a "major public health concern." Loneliness has been scientifically linked to other risks such as higher blood pressure, body mass index, cholesterol levels, depression and early mortality with rates similar to those found with obesity or smoking fifteen cigarettes a day!

While the previous generation, those 72 and older, had more natural ways of relating (think living closer to extended family, religious functions, neighborhood potlucks), many of those practices fell by the wayside as America moved into the 21st century. My parents grew up in a small farm town in Iowa. I remember my father telling me how his parents would gather at a different farm house every weekend to play cards with their neighbors while the kids played together. Today as I raise my children, I don't even know most of my neighbors.

Our loneliness as a nation is only increasing. And it shows. No matter how much we love or hate it, the truth is that we need each other. It's the way God made us. It cannot be avoided. Whether it be through immediate family, marriage, church groups, co-workers, or community gatherings, we need fellowship. We need to be known and to know others. Especially in times of crisis, we need help.

In Luke's Gospel, he tells the story about a time when Jesus was teaching in the house of one of the religious leaders:

"Some men took a man who was not able to move his body to Jesus. He was carried on a bed. They looked for a way to take the man into the house where Jesus was. But they could not find a way to take him in because of so many people. They made a

hole in the roof over where Jesus stood. Then they let the b
with the sick man on it down before Jesus. When Jesus saw th
faith, He said to the man, 'Friend, your sins are forgiven.'
Luke 5:18-20

What catches my attention in this passage is how Jesus sa *their* faith. It doesn't say he saw the faith of the man who wa crippled and lying on the bed. He saw the faith of the man' *friends*. And that was the faith Jesus used to heal the man.

Some people will say that you need faith personally to see your mountains move, and I agree with them in general. Most of our struggles are wrestled out with God on a personal level. We have not because we ask not. But this story proves that this is not *always* the case. Had this man given up hope? Did he believe he could be healed? Clearly he couldn't get to Jesus on his own, so his friends carried him. Did he want to go? I don't know the answers to these questions. The Bible doesn't tell us. It does tell us though that the friends had the faith to bring him all the way to Jesus, cut a hole in some poor guy's roof, and dangle their friend in front of Jesus. I wonder if Jesus was mildly amused. (I also wonder if the home owners had insurance.)

There have been times in my life when I did not have the strength or the faith to ask for what I needed. I mean, I was asking, but I had lost the "oomph" that was required to push through. I remember in those times the way that friends and family carried me through on their prayers. The first time was when I was carrying our son, the rainbow baby I previously mentioned. I was so afraid that I was going to lose him even though I was desperately trying to hang onto God's promises.

At one point during the first trimester, we were scheduled to attend leaders gathering in the home of our mission's directors. I wasn't able to be there for all of the meetings, but the one prayer meeting that I showed up for, our director asked everyone to gather around me and pray. They prayed for our son, growing in my womb. They prayed strength and health for me. They prayed for faith for Rich and I. They stood against fear. They received words and pictures from the Holy Spirit that they shared with us so that we could be encouraged. They got God's heart for us and released it, and there was a shift in the spirit. It's real, folks. Intercession, praying God's Kingdom into existence on behalf of another person, can change futures!

God is looking for people to "stand in the gap" for others (Ezekiel 22:30). And he calls others to stand with us in our time of need. Of course, Jesus is our great intercessor. He took our place when we had no way of helping ourselves. And he calls us to help others through prayer and practical works.

I am so grateful for all of the meals prepared, gift cards sent, and hours spent caring for my children or cleaning my house as I went through chemo and surgeries and radiation. I could not have done it by myself. My husband definitely could not have done it alone.

Not too long into treatment, my hospital's oncologist social worker recommended that I tell my children's teachers about what was going on in case the kids were processing my diagnosis there at school as well. I'm so glad I did even if only to save my own dignity because I'm sure they would have known something was going down when my son showed up to school in the middle of winter wearing only a t-shirt with underwear that he hadn't changed in three days and fingernails

that had gone unclipped since the fall. Or my daughter who went to school in a dress two sizes too small for her with the bum of her tights hanging out and a rat's nest on top of her head. She told us that she eventually had to explain to her kindergarten bestie that her hair often looked like this because "my dad forgets to brush it in the morning sometimes." Sweet child. I am sorry. But the kids survived and so did we. (And the teachers never called Child Protective Services on us thanks to the advice of a wise social worker!)

The Trinity of Community

We were created in the image of God, so we need community to flourish. God himself dwells in the plural. In his very being, there is community. It is not just God the Father by himself on his throne. It is and always has been God, the three-in-one. God the Father, God the Son, and God the Holy Spirit. It is still somewhat of a mystery to me. The apple peel, fruit, and core analogy didn't fully do the trick in Sunday School to explain this triune God, yet this is the truth of his nature. And this is the truth of our nature as well. Through Jesus, we are brought into the holy trinity. We become a part of God's community. We are not God, but we can become one with him. We see this in Jesus' final prayer for us before he went to the cross:

"'I am not asking on behalf of them (the disciples) *alone, but also on behalf of those who will believe in Me through their message, that all of them may be one as You, Father, are in Me, and I am in You. **May they also be in Us**, so that the world may believe that You sent Me.'*

*I have given them the glory You gave me, so that they may be one **as We are one-** I in them and You in Me- that they may be perfectly united, so that the world may know that You sent Me and **have loved them just as You have loved Me.***"
John 17:20-21

Wow! There's a lot to unpack there. It has always been God's desire that we are in him. He created us for perfect fellowship with himself. Our ultimate fulfillment comes in *being loved by God.* Yes, we are meant to love him in return, but we are built to be a dwelling place for the love of our Father. I always feel a bit nervous when a woman says that she wants a baby because she wants to be loved by someone. It seems backwards to me. It should be that we have children because we want to share *our love* with someone else, not because we need to be loved. This is the right and natural order because this is how God is. We intrinsically know this because we were made in his image.

God created us because he wanted to love us. When we broke relationship with him, he made a way for that relationship to be restored. We love because he first loved us (1 John 4:19). We cannot love well without being loved. We cannot pour out without first being filled up. We must know and receive his love before we can love others.

In John 14:15, Jesus says, "If you love me, you will keep my commands." For so many years I read that statement as a goal to be attained. I tried my best to "keep his commands" and prove my love for him. It wasn't until I heard a wise teacher explain that these words of Jesus are *descriptive* rather than *prescriptive*. Jesus was not saying, "If you really love me, you'll work extra hard to do what I say." He already knew we couldn't do it. We don't make the cut. Thousands of years of human history already made that very clear. If we could have kept his commands on our own, why would he even have come to earth? (I'm sure it wasn't for the food.) He knew we would need his Spirit to keep those commands.

Rather Jesus is saying, "If you love me, you'll naturally keep my commands." Don't worry about it! If you love someone, you naturally want to please them! You don't have to work at it. True, sometimes it doesn't feel so nice to choose love over selfish gratification, but the more that I get to know Jesus and experience his deep, overwhelming love for me, the more I want to love him in return. When I hear his kind words or experience his gentle ways, when I understand again and again how he gave up everything for me, it is not difficult to lay my life down for him. It even becomes less difficult to lay down my life for others.

My husband is a very gracious person. He is more gentle and patient by nature than I am, but shortly after we married, we began to argue. Yes, it's true, two missionaries in conflict. We still argue now sometimes, but these newlywed arguments were different. The honeymoon phase had worn off, and I saw another side to him that I had somehow missed in the rose-colored haze, as I'm sure he had with me. There was one particular time that I was especially mad at him. I honestly don't remember what it was now, but I do remember that *he* was at fault and was being exceptionally unreasonable. He was clearly the one in the wrong and should be the first to apologize. I had done no (or at least very little) harm, so it would not be fair for me to take the blame.

I was holding my position. I decided that I was not going to budge on this one, but kind and wise Holy Spirit began to tug on my heart. I explained my position to him. He agreed, Richard had done wrong. "Ha! I knew it!" I thought. But Holy Spirit also wondered what part I had played in the fiasco. I explained again that surely the little stick in my eye didn't compare to the log in my husband's. Maybe, but I still felt nudged to apologize for my part. "He doesn't deserve it!" I sputtered. *"Then do it for me. Do I deserve it?"* the Holy Spirit whispered. Oh man. That was below the belt, Lord. There was only one way to answer that question. Yes, of course God deserves it. He is worthy of me choosing to forgive and be gracious even when someone else does not. So I went and apologized, (and my husband did in return) and the relationship was mended. Not because my husband was deserving due to his actions, but because Jesus always is.

The above verses in John 17 show us that it is completely possible for us to live in total unity with other believers. Jesus would not have prayed for it if it were impossible. On the other hand, he must have realized the magnitude of his request because he mentioned it to the Father in his last hours on earth. Unity is totally possible *but only with the help of the Holy Spirit.* As humans, we need each other. As Christians, we need each other even more. And the world needs us to be unified. John 17:21 says "'that they may be perfectly united, so that the world may know that You sent Me *and have loved them just as You have loved Me.*'" It is not just for our own sake. It is also for the sake of those that do not yet know Jesus. Our unity, the love that we have for each other, is what proves to the world that Jesus was sent by the Father.

In Romans 12:10, we are instructed to, "Love each other with genuine affection, and take delight in honoring each other." This kind of love has to be *supernatural.* We cannot naturally love everyone in this manner. It's actually *unnatural* to love people that we don't even know or people that we don't like. The standard is set so high that it requires supernatural help.

Quite a few years ago, I was working on a small team with a large non-profit organization. It was just a handful of us working on a particular project, so we saw A LOT of each other. There was nowhere to run and nowhere to hide. And there was one coworker in particular who really got on my nerves and under my skin. This person was extremely detail-oriented and would take up so much of our time asking (what I considered to be) irrelevant and unnecessary questions. She got irritated easily and would lose her temper at times, and she didn't make up for it with an interesting or fun personality. She was fairly dull to be around.

Now, this was all my *perspective*. It felt like reality but in truth, this person was made in the image of God. God loved my coworker and found her just as amazing as he did me. The problem was that I was making it all about myself. Without realizing it, I had put conditions on the love that I would give. I needed to feel a certain way about a person before I felt I could love them or enjoy their company. I didn't want to be around this person because I felt they didn't add anything to my life.

I shared this with my director one day because I was really struggling. My director asked if I had been praying for this person? No, not really. She suggested that I spend time every day praying blessings for this person and asking God to give me his heart and his eyes for my coworker (so *not* praying for God to change my coworker). She also suggested that I begin to pursue a friendship with this person. Ugh. I really didn't want to do that, but I was beginning to realize that this was more my problem than anyone else's. God did not say to love only the people who I deem worthy of my love. He said to love everyone, and to do it from the heart.

Well, sometimes you need to fake it to make it, right? So I began to heed my director's suggestions and started praying for this coworker. I stepped out in faith and asked her out to coffee. I made a decision to lay down my "right" to be mutually encouraged or entertained by someone else and decided just to be a blessing even if I didn't feel like I was getting anything out of it. God didn't say I had to be best friends with everyone, but I did need to learn to authentically love those who were different to me.

After a time of praying for and pursuing this person, an amazing transformation began to take place. As I asked for God to give me his heart for her and began to intentionally spend time with her, I found that she wasn't so boring after all. She must have become more interesting! I began to see her as a whole person with hopes and dreams, fears and hurts. I learned about her family and her past. I began to have *compassion,* and as my compassion grew, so did my friendship with this coworker. All the icky feelings I had began to melt away as I determined to move in the opposite direction of my emotions and towards the standard that I knew God wanted me to live at. And I found true freedom.

No longer do I need to like someone to be able to love them. No longer am I bound by the chains of having my own personal ego stroked or needing someone to be amusing/interesting/ charming/intelligent/well-spoken/conservative/liberal before I can love them. I can love anyone because I can see them through God's eyes if I ask him for that vision.

This is what Jesus means when he speaks of being a servant. I can serve people by befriending them, by honoring and valuing them even if I don't think they are adding value to my life (when in fact they are). I can lay down my own agenda and rights to feel a certain way when I'm with others and simply give my time and my love to another human being. But it requires supernatural help. We can't do it alone, or at least we can't sustain it for very long. It is possible though because God's love sets us free to love others without needing anything in return. Just like he loves us.

Same Spirit, Different Styles

In all of my travels to various countries around the world, to different cultures and church denominations with multiple styles of worship and numerous versions of the Bible in multiple languages, the one common thread is the Spirit of Christ within us. No matter where I go, when I am with other believers, I am at home *because we share the same Spirit.* Some churches shout prayers loudly while others whisper. Some raise their hands while others keep theirs folded. Some dance and others sit. Some specialize in prophesy and others in potlucks. Some meet in houses and others in stadiums. Some sing a capella and others have a full choir with electric guitars. But you know the most beautiful thing is? I have seen God move in every one of those churches.

I am continually amazed at how humble the Holy Spirit is. He comes to us in the ways that our customs and traditions have explained him to come, in the ways that we expect him to come. Do some churches limit him? Yes, actually they ALL do. There is *no church on earth* that does not somehow limit God. There is no church on earth that has the right answer and the perfect method for everything. In fact, I believe that God gives different revelation and understanding to different churches and denominations *so that* we always need each other if we want to have the full picture of who he is.

Want some powerful group worship? Try the Charismatic bunch. Need some solid teaching? See the Baptists. Help on how to grow in discipline? Try the Methodists. Desire to feel accepted in the Body? Look to the Presbyterians. It's not that one group has ownership over any one area, but we clearly have our own strengths, just as siblings do in a family. How often do I tell my children to encourage each other when one of them succeeds instead of comparing? Doesn't God feel the same about his kids?

*"There are different gifts, but the **same Spirit**. There are different ministries, but the **same Lord**. There are different ways of working, but the **same God** works all things in all men. Now to each one the manifestations of the Spirit **is given for the common good**...The body is a unit, though it is comprised of many parts. And although its parts are many, they all form **one body**. So it is with Christ."*
1 Corinthians 12:4-12

We are all going to be in the afterlife together anyway, so we might as well work it out here. And really the tragic part is that the world misses out on seeing Jesus when we choose division over unity. *We will never agree on everything!* Never! I suppose we aren't even meant to. That is what true diversity means. We must all carry a certain amount of humility when encountering those outside of our own "fold" and forever entertain the possibility that we might be the ones in the wrong. Most of us are really trying to follow Jesus to the best of our abilities. If you find that you have stronger faith than another, then adjust yourself to the level they are on and don't put any stumbling blocks in their way. And if you discover that you are the one struggling to understand, accept that fact that you don't have it all together and might be missing it somewhere as well. *We all are.* People can study the Scriptures and come to different conclusions. They are not accountable to us. They are accountable to God, just as we are. And he can direct them to what is true, just as he does with us.

Some of what I believed to be true twenty years ago I now realize was just human tradition. I just didn't know at the time. Does that mean I didn't love Jesus twenty years ago? No! It just means that I didn't yet have the full understanding in those areas. And it's very possible that in another twenty years some of what I believe to be true now will no longer have a place in my life. That is good. That is called growth. I would be more concerned if my theology never changed. It must change if we are growing and seeing God in newer and truer ways. We can only live according to the *light that we have already received.* We cannot live according to light that we *will* receive or light that *someone else* has received. Only what God has shown us to be true. That is what we are accountable for.

Many will tell you not to put God in a box, but recently a friend of ours shared that he believes God lives in our boxes. We all have God in a box, somehow or another because we all have a limited understanding of who he is. God is not too concerned with our boxes. He crawls into them with us so that he can love us. When we are ready, he enlarges the boxes' walls and stretches their corners so that there is more room within them.

More room for him, for us, and for others. He is Emmanuel, God in the flesh.

I have found that God meets people where they are at. He desires for us to hear him more than we want it for ourselves. Whether that be through the Bible to a new Christian, in a dream to a Buddhist monk asking for the Way, in a vision to a Muslim praying to know the Truth, or to an atheist who tangibly encounters the presence of God and cannot explain it away, God is headstrong on revealing Jesus to us! *God wants to be known!* He is committed to reaching us despite our most fortified attempts to shelter ourselves. He wants us to know him and is continually inviting us to a larger Story than our own.

Living in community helps us to grow beyond our own personal (and limited) boxes. We learn from each other. We grow with each other. We can lean on each other. God made us this way. We were not meant to be islands. In this walk of faith, it is important to have others to inspire and encourage us on. We need it as much as they do. So let us pray that we would all be filled with the supernatural love that covers over faults so that we can experience true unity.

Chapter Seven

WORSHIPPING IN THE VALLEY

"Though the fig tree does not bud
and no fruit is on the vines,
though the olive crop fails
and the fields produce no food,
though the sheep are cut off from the fold
and no cattle are in the stalls,
yet I will exult in the LORD; I will rejoice
in the God of my salvation!"

Habakkuk 3:17-18

From Miracle to Despair

When we think of the prophet Elijah, visions of greatness come to mind. Very few others in the Bible saw the supernatural power of God in the way that he did. But when we catch him in 1 Kings 19, we see the prophet in a different state. He is hiding out in a cave just after one of the most dramatic, powerful encounters recorded in the Bible between God and the prophets of Baal. God had totally showed up on behalf of Elijah's prayers and demonstrated his strength and supremacy by causing fire to come and consume an altar that had been drenched in water multiple times. The people were astounded.

After this, Elijah prophesies that rain is coming on Israel's drought-stricken land. God responds once again to Elijah's prayers and sends the rain. But shortly after these incredible moves of God, Israel's wicked queen, Jezebel, is informed of what Elijah has done and makes a pact to kill him. So although Elijah has JUST SEEN the power of God displayed in incredible force, he is overcome with fear and runs for his life.

A few verses later, he is hiding out in a cave in the middle of nowhere. There, the word of the Lord finally comes to him and asks, "What are you doing here, Elijah?" Elijah explains how he has been zealous for the Lord, but the Israelites have not responded the way he hoped. He goes on and tells the Lord how they have torn down his altars and killed his prophets and now they are looking to kill him too. The Lord doesn't respond to Elijah's comments directly but tells him to go out and stand on the mountain in his presence because he is going to pass by.

Then a great and powerful wind passes by and shatters the rocks, tearing the mountain apart, but the Lord was not in the wind. Next, an earthquake occurs, shaking the land, but the Lord was not in the earthquake. Finally, a fire breaks out, burning the area, but the Lord was not in the fire. After the fire came a gentle whisper. When Elijah hears it, he pulls his cloak over his face and stands at the mouth of the cave.

Again the Lord asks him, "What are you doing here, Elijah?" And again Elijah responds in the same manner. The Lord proceeds to instruct Elijah to return the way that he came and as he goes, to anoint two men: one who will be the next king and one who will succeed Elijah as God's prophet. "And by the way, Elijah," God adds, "you are not actually the only prophet left like you think you are. There are 7,000 others who have not bowed to Baal either."

Hard times have a way of distorting what is true. When we face challenges in life, it is difficult to see it all in context. Even though Elijah knew that God was powerful and able to protect him, he still became afraid and ran away from his enemies. God did not chastise Elijah. Instead he sustained him along the way, allowed him to hide out in a cave, demonstrated his power yet again, and finally gently called Elijah out. He could see that Elijah needed help, so he assigned Elisha to be his mentee and Jehu to be the next righteous king. He also corrected Elijah's fake news and revealed that there were, in fact, many other prophets who were still living for God, just as Elijah was.

I have heard it said that we should not lower the standard of God's Word to fit our experiences, but we should work to *raise our experiences* to the standard of this Word. Just because we do not receive what we are asking for every time, even when we believe it's what God wants, it does not mean that we should stop asking. We must be very careful, especially after great disappointment, to guard our hearts from resentment and bitterness. In these times of distress, it is easy to entertain accusations against God's character. It doesn't take much for us to begin to doubt God's goodness and his ability or his willingness to come through for us when life isn't going well. We can lose sight of what he's done in the past and forget the promises that he's made for our future.

In the well-loved Christian classic, *The Pilgrim's Progress* we see the hero of the story, a man named Christian, on a long journey from his hometown, the City of Destruction to his destination, the Celestial City. At one point in the story, he is traveling with a companion, Hopeful, when they are captured by the Giant Despair and thrown into a dungeon located in Doubting Castle. Once locked inside their cell, they are beaten repeatedly. One morning, they are taken to a spot in the castle where the bones of past pilgrims lay scattered on the ground. They see the remains of sojourners who had come before them yet never escaped this fortress of doubt.

Despite the physical and mental assault, Christian and Hopeful refuse to give up. One night, Christian suddenly realizes a way for them to escape and passionately explains what he has discovered:

> *"'What a fool,' quoth he, 'am I, thus to lie in a stinking dungeon, when I may as well walk at liberty! I have a key in my bosom called Promise; that will, I am persuaded, open any lock in Doubting Castle.'"*

Hopeful encourages him to try the key and hallelujah-hooray, the key works! Every heavy door and iron gate in the castle can be unlocked with this key of Promise! The two go on to escape from the Doubting Castle and continue on their journey.

As I mentioned, there is *often* a waiting period between the time the promise is given and the moment it is fulfilled. In fact almost *every single* promise in the Bible required God's people to wait until he made his word a reality. Just think about it: the first promise of a coming redemption made in the Garden of Eden just after Adam and Eve got the world's first eviction notice, the promise to Abraham that his descendants would be the like the stars in the sky even though he was elderly and his wife was barren, the promise made to the Israelites that they would be delivered out of Egypt when they had been slaves for hundreds of years, and the promise given to the various prophets of the Old Testament that a Messiah would one day be born to rescue his people. Even the resurrection of Jesus himself required a waiting period.

Don't think for a moment that any *one* of those disciples was full of faith in the three days between his death and Easter Sunday! And finally us, the Bride of Christ, waiting for his return and the restoration of all things, the last promise fulfilled. It is in this waiting that faith must hold, because it is in this waiting that it will be severely tested.

If all of God's promises were answered immediately, there would be no need for persevering faith. It is in these times when all seems lost, with no sight of land on the horizon, that we are told to trust. Hopelessness does not exist in God's Kingdom. If there's any area of our lives that feels hopeless, then it's not yet come into the light of Jesus' reign. Our God is a God of hope. He is a way-maker. There is nothing beyond his reach, no realm outside of his ability to change. Even if we are in the waiting period of faith, if he has spoken it, he will bring it to pass because he is faithful.

The Waiting Room

So what do we do in the waiting? I'll tell you what I do (and what many heroes of the faith did in the Bible). I look to God. I focus on who he is and what he's like. I lift him up. It can look a little bit like this:

This is me represented by a dot: .
This is my enemy represented by a zero: 0
Here we are side by side: . 0

Clearly my enemy is much bigger than I am. The cancer, the depression, the marital breakdown, the prodigal daughter, whatever it may be. There's no way that this little dot can take on that zero and win. And no dot in her right mind would even try it.

But here is God represented by zeroes:
0000000000000000000000000000000000000000000000000
0000000000000000000000000000000000000000000000000
0000000000000000000000000000000000000000000000000
0000000000000000000000000000000000000000000000000
0000000000000000000000000000000000000000000000000
0000000000000000000000000000000000000000000000000
00000000000000000000000000000000000 (x infinite)

Now compare that one little enemy zero "0" to the many zeroes that represent God. Somehow the lone zero doesn't seem so big anymore. We must lift up our eyes to see the God who encompasses the heavens, set the planets in motion, and created galaxies we will probably never even know about until our afterlives. And then our problems won't seem so big.

Not only is he powerful, but he is faithful. Joshua and Caleb, two of the spies who saw the giants, more importantly saw the God who created the entire earth, the One who said that he was going to give them the land. They believed God and because of that they were able to take hold of what was promised to them. The other ten did not believe and missed out. Did God not want to give the land to them too? Yes, of course. Did he like Joshua and Caleb more? Of course not. The promise was for everyone, *but most of them didn't enter in.*

These are the same spies who saw God do crazy-mad miracles. They had no reason to doubt that God could do it. We live in a time and place where many of us have never even seen one teeny-tiny little supernatural act. But I bet if we took time to look over our lives, we would see God's hand in it. We must start there.

Little Altars Everywhere

There are many times recorded in the Bible where God tells his people to build an altar of remembrance, a memorial that would help them recall what he had done for them. God knew how fickle and forgetful the Israelites were, how all consuming their challenges became when they were in the midst of them, so he provided a practical way for the Israelites to get out of that crazy anxiety-cycle by turning their focus to remember the ways that he had provided for and protected them in the past. And this memorial was not just for them. It would also serve the generations that would come after them, those who may have not yet seen the moves of God.

We see an example of this in the book of Joshua, just after God has parted the Jordan River to bring his people into the Promised Land (finally).

"So Joshua called together the twelve men he had appointed from the Israelites, one from each tribe, and said to them, 'Go over before the ark of the Lord your God into the middle of the Jordan. Each of you is to take up a stone on his shoulder, according to the number of the tribes of the Israelites, to serve as a sign among you. In the future, when your children ask you, "What do these stones mean?" tell them that the flow of the Jordan was cut off before the ark of the covenant of the Lord. When it crossed the Jordan, the waters of the Jordan were cut off. These stones are to be a memorial to the people of Israel forever.'"
Joshua 4:4-7

They were told to take large rocks from the *middle of the dry path* that God had carved in the Jordan River and set them up as remembrance stones. What are our remembrance stones? What do we use to remind ourselves of what God has done in the past? What do we point our children to when they ask about God's faithfulness?

I have stories, times I recount where God spoke a promise to me and then he kept it. Some stories I've told so many times that I will never forget them. Other stories I write down in a notebook because I don't want to forget. Along with the stories, I write down the words that God has spoken to me, verses that secure what he will do. I have an arsenal of memories to share with friends and family, to remind myself when doubt creeps in, and even declare to the enemy when I feel him pressing: a hike I went on when God promised to give me a husband, a word that came from a friend when God encouraged me to be bolder, a verse that dropped into my mind during a midnight prayer session on a rooftop in Asia that promised to bring my team safely out of the country, a dream that came in the early morning and brought me word of God's coming deliverance. I recall these moments and my faith is strengthened.

My parents had stories like these as well. Memories that I treasured hearing about. How they met Jesus, how he led them to jobs and homes and friends, how he healed them, how he redeemed relationships and kept our family from harm. We need these stories. In Revelation 12:11, we read, "They have conquered him (the accuser) by the blood of the Lamb and the *word of their testimony*." Our testimonies are powerful weapons that we can use to stand against the enemy and to build ourselves up.

We need to remember and record all of the times that God has been faithful to us in the past. Ask the Holy Spirit to help bring them to mind. Walk yourself through the years and try to recall what was happening during those times and what God did for you. This will increase your confidence.

It will also increase your gratitude.

Gratitude is another key component of learning to worship in the valley. Whenever a situation feels hopeless, disciplining ourselves to look for the good means that our perspectives will change. A study[10] about the power of gratitude was performed on nearly three hundred adults who were all seeking some kind of mental health counseling, mainly for depression and anxiety. The participants were randomly assigned into three groups. All of the groups received counseling, but the three groups had slightly different assignments during those weeks of therapy.

The first group was instructed to write one letter of gratitude to someone else each week for three weeks. The second group was asked to write their honest thoughts and feelings in regards to their negative experiences. The third group was the control group and had no writing assignments. At the end of the study, the researchers followed up with all of the participants. They found that compared with those who had only received counseling or had written about their negative experiences, the group who wrote gratitude letters reported *significantly better* mental health four weeks and twelve weeks after the writing assignments finished.

The researchers went on to make these four conclusions based on further information that they had received from the participants about gratitude: 1. Gratitude unshackles us from toxic emotions, 2. Gratitude helps even if you don't share it, 3. Gratitude's benefits take time, 4. Gratitude has lasting effects on the brain.[11]

God hard-wired us with a need to be thankful. The storms of life can threaten to diminish that desire, but we can choose gratitude even in the midst of difficult times. And when we do, we'll find our spirits actually lift. Science even proves it!

(An excellent resource on this topic of gratitude is Ann Voskamp's book *One Thousand Gifts*.)

Just Admit It

One very important step that we must take if we are weenies is to admit that we are. When we look at David in the Bible, we don't usually associate him with being a weenie, but if you spend any time at all in the Psalms, you'll see that he clearly was. And he was not afraid to admit it!

David is often found telling the Lord that he's afraid, that he is grieved, that he needs help. These are the confessions of humility. What David does not do though is stop there. He freely admits that he is not capable of doing what needs to be done, and then he looks to the One who can do it.

In 1 Samuel 30, while David and his men were out battling the Philistines, the Amalekites raided their hometown and captured their wives, families, and possessions. (This was also during the time when David was already an outlaw in Israel due to the breakdown in relationship between him and King Saul, so not a good time for David.) When David and his men returned to their town and discovered what had happened, they were devastated. The men turned on David, blamed him for what went down, and even wanted to kill him. The Bible tells us that David then took some time and "strengthened himself in the Lord."

David did not possess the courage and wisdom needed for each situation that he faced. But he knew the *source* of all courage and wisdom. And he was smart (or maybe desperate) enough to ask for help. After his time with the Lord, he knew what to do. The Lord gave him a plan that would rescue their families and possessions.

This is what the Scripture means when it says in Isaiah 40:31, "Those who wait on the Lord shall RENEW their strength." Strength can be gained or lost. When we take time to wait on God, our strength is restored.

This has happened countless times in my walk with God. Times of desperation with my kids or my husband or my job or my health where I felt I had nothing else to give. Fear and anxiety threatened to overtake me. The circumstances seemed too much to bear. I didn't have a thousand burly men wanting to kill me like David did, but it kind of felt like it.

I've been asked what it looks like to wait on the Lord. What does that even mean? Well, it can look different for different people. For me, it often means closing myself in my room ALONE, putting on worship music, and focusing on Jesus. I take my eyes off the giants in my life and put them back on the One who can take care of those beasts. I remind myself of the truth. That he's able, that he's trustworthy, that he cares, that he's with me, that he'll supply wisdom and strength as I need them.

We will never outgrow this need to wait on God. We will never mature enough to no longer depend upon it. We were not made to do it alone. We were made to walk together with God. We were made with limited brains and bodies and hearts. We need God to compensate for our limitations.

At some stage on the journey in seeing healing from the cancer in my body, I was discouraged and feeling overwhelmed as I looked at all the various treatments and procedures that still needed to be done. I didn't know if I was strong enough. I didn't know if I could do it. I definitely didn't want to. I shut myself in a room alone with God and poured out my heart to him. I told him that I was sad. That it was unfair. That I was angry. That I was scared. I put some worship music on and lifted up my eyes towards him. In my anguish, I heard the whisper, "Psalm 46," in my heart, so I turned there and found this gem in verse five:

*"God is our refuge and our strength, a very present
help in times of trouble...
God is within her. SHE WILL NOT FALL. God will
help her at break of day."*

Those were the words I needed to hear. That WORD gave me life. God was promising me that I would not fall, that no matter what came, he himself would help me. He was reminding me of his commitment. At that moment, the burdens fell off. My circumstances had not changed one iota, but I had shifted in my stance. I remembered that I was not walking alone. In a world where we're told we must pull ourselves up by our bootstraps, God was saying that I did not have to muster the strength by myself. It would be given, at the right time, when I needed it the most. God would help me, and I would not fall. I clung to that promise in the months after.

I just cannot stress enough how important praise is in the battles of life. It's guaranteed that we will all have more hardships to face along this road. No matter how hard I try to weatherproof my life so that no further pain seeps in, it's inevitable. I will face situations that will be too much for me to bear on my own. I will either break under their weight or I will find my strength in the Lord.

God doesn't need to be praised. He is full in himself. We are the ones who *need to praise*. He's given us that gift to focus on and lift up a Being greater than ourselves. As we do this, we realize it's not about us. And it's not about our difficult circumstances. As we magnify him (make him bigger in our own minds and hearts), we are the ones who change.

You can see this over and over in the psalms. David writes
about how hard life is and about how he feels. About his
despair. But he always ends with "BUT GOD." But God is
bigger. But God is able. But God is faithful. This is the truth
that sets us free from our burdens. This is the truth that
strengthens our hearts. This is what we need to know.

Our feelings and our circumstances and our pain and our
emptiness is not the end. They do not have to have the final
word. God can come down and meet us in the pit and lift us up
to a higher place, a place where we can see with his perspective.
Compared to the heavens, the 8-foot giant will no longer seem
so tall.

Do It Afraid

We can trust in the Lord and still *feel* scared. We can trust in the
Lord and at the same time call a spade a spade. When the doctor
told me I had cancer, I didn't pretend that I didn't. I just went
back to Jesus and said, "What's your word?" And once I got
that, it was the final word. Did I doubt it at times? Heck, yes.
It's a battle to believe. But the more I fought to hang onto his
promise, the less it fought back until it wasn't much of a fight at
all. I was convinced that God would do what he said that he
would do. He'd never let me down before. Nelson Mandela
once said:

> *"I learned that courage was not the absence of fear, but the
> triumph over it. The brave man is not he who does not feel
> afraid, but he who conquers that fear."*

Sometimes what we need is not more faith but more courage. I often pray like the early Christians in Acts did, that God would "stretch out his hand and make me bold." We need a righteous anger against sickness and brokenness, against the enemy's attempts to steal what God wants us and others to have. We see this healthy anger when David approaches Goliath. "Who is this heathen Philistine that he should defy the armies of the living God," David defiantly questions in 1 Samuel 17:26. We need to take a little more of the "oomph" that we feel when someone cuts us off in traffic and direct towards our true enemies.

Fear's purpose is immobilization, but *anger is a call towards action.* When we are fed up enough with getting pounded by the waves, we'll either give up or we'll find a way to conquer them. (I'm talking about hypothetical waves here. I'm way too afraid to try surfing.) We can tap into the energy that anger provides and use it to keep on going. I'm not talking about some mystic, cosmic energy. I mean the actual, real energy you feel when you are mad. It makes you want to do something! That is the point of anger. We usually see it as a negative emotion, but God made it. It doesn't have to lead towards sin. If I saw some bully trying to harm my child, I would feel angry. That anger makes me step in and stop what's happening. If I only felt sadness, I would be less prone to do anything about it.

We should feel angry when we see people living in disease and poverty. God does! I wonder just how many inventions and interventions over the course of history started with someone getting mad about something. Dr. Martin Luther King Jr. inspired tens of thousands to turn their anger into peaceful protest. The women's suffrage amendment to the U.S. Constitution was passed in the early 1900s because enough women were fed up with the injustice of being denied a right to vote. And even discoveries like pasteurization were birthed in Louis Pasteur's anger towards the victors in a war with his beloved France.[12]

One of the most-watched VHS videos in my house growing up was the original 1984 version of the film, *Red Dawn*. If you were not as fortunate as I to have experienced childhood before the PG-13 rating was well-known, or if your parents tried to protect you from traumatic memories, let me recap it for you.

The movie tells the story of a band of teenagers whose hometown in Colorado (along with the rest of the US) has been invaded by the Soviet Union. (I swear my brother was digging fox holes with his best friend as a side effect of this movie well into the 90s.) We see the young clan mature from a bunch of scared kids into brave soldiers. And though this movie brings up all of the nostalgic feels for me, I wouldn't necessarily take a lot of life advice from it, Except for maybe a few scenes, this one included:

Two of the teenagers, Jed and Matty (played by Patrick Swayze and Charlie Sheen) are brothers. The Soviets have just killed their father in a prison camp, and his final wish was for his boys to avenge him. The boys are now back at their hideout in the mountains, grieving the loss of their dad when the younger one, Matty begins to cry. Jed responds to him saying, "Don't cry. Hold it back. Let it turn to something else. Just let it turn to something else." We go onto see Matty taking his older brother's advice. The pain did turn to something else, and it fueled the courage he needed to eventually give up his life in defense of his country and his family.

I'm not saying it's always the best advice not to cry and let your emotions out. *I cry.* I cry a lot, in fact. But there is a time and place to say enough is enough, wipe the tears off your face, and put your cowboy boots on because it's game time. The enemy came to steal, kill, and destroy, but he didn't realize who he was messing with. You may just be equipped with a sling and a few stones, but you're backed by all the chariots of heaven because your Daddy is the King. And this King don't put up with anyone messing with his child.

Chapter Eight

WHAT'S IN YOUR HAND?

"The journey of a thousand miles begins with a single step."

Lao Tzu

If You've Got It, Flaunt It

After I was diagnosed with cancer, I tried really hard to believe that it would just go away without any treatment. I was terrified of the thought of chemo and radiation. I decided I would pray and trust that God would supernaturally heal me until the deadline of the next MRI scan, where the doctors were going to determine if the cancer had spread and what course of action was necessary. I prayed. I declared. I quoted scripture. Deep down, I knew that I was going to be okay because I had that promise from the Lord, but I didn't know which way my healing was going to come. I desperately wanted it to be one hundred percent supernatural because it was the quickest and most pain-free way. But the healing didn't come at that point.

The MRI showed the cancer was still in my breast and had spread to some lymph nodes. Chemotherapy was to be the first and next step. It was recommend I have a port placed near my right shoulder in two days to make IVs easier to bear during the upcoming months.

Would I have been supernaturally healed if I had had more faith? It's possible. I know of people who have seen it happen. Like I mentioned previously, I believe if Jesus would have been beside me in bodily form, I would have been healed on the spot. The Bible tells us that everyone who came to Jesus asking for healing was healed- right there. Done and dusted. Everyone who *asked* him was totally healed. And I had been asking. But what if you're a weenie faith?

After much deliberation, I decided just to admit to Jesus what he already knew. I was a wimp. I only had a little bit of faith. I did not have enough to see my healing come supernaturally even though I desperately wanted to. So God in his mercy said, "What's in your hand?"

When God called Moses to go back to Egypt and tell Pharaoh to let the Israelites go, Moses was totally freaked out, and rightfully so. Pharaoh had the power to eliminate Moses on the spot. Moses made excuses as to why he was not the man for the job. God humored him and made allowance for his fear, going through the exact steps that he needed to take to free his people from slavery and lead them into their Promised Land, but Moses still had questions. How would the Israelites (and Pharaoh) know that God was with him? Why would they listen to him? God responded by asking Moses a question of his own, "What's in your hand?"

A staff. Moses had an ordinary shepherd's staff in his hand. God told him to throw the staff down on the ground and it became a snake, one supernatural sign that God was with him. Moses also had a hand. God told him to put his hand in his cloak. When he took it out, it was leprous- another supernatural sign that God was with him. After a couple more of these confirmations, Moses was still fearful and told the Lord that he was not good at making speeches, especially not in front of powerful rulers. God was not pleased. He corrected Moses but still mercifully allowed his brother, Aaron to go with him to help him.

God used what Moses already had, a simple shepherd's staff, to execute a grand exodus for the entire nation of Israel. Did God need the staff? Of course not, but he used what Moses had on hand to bring about his purposes. God is so humble that he's willing to operate within our limitations. He graciously gives us physical and practical steps of faith to do that will encourage us and increase our faith, thus accomplishing his purposes for us in the end.

One beautiful example of this is found in 2 Kings 4 with the prophet Elijah and the widow's empty jars. A widow approaches Elijah and explains her situation: her husband (who was also in the company of prophets) has died and a creditor is coming to take her two sons as slaves because she has nothing else with which she can pay him back. Elijah asks her a very similar question to the one that God asked Moses, "What do you have in your house?"

"Nothing," she replies, "except a small jar of olive oil." Elijah proceeds to instruct her to gather as many jars as she can find from all of her neighbors, not just a few but many! Once she has them, she is to return to her home with her sons and privately fill each jar with olive oil from the jar she has on hand. So that's just what she did. She filled each and every jar from that one little container of olive oil until there were no more jars to be filled. When she returned to tell Elijah all that happened, he told her to sell the olive oil and pay off her debts.

I love that story! God takes what we have and makes it enough. In both of these examples, with Moses and the widow, God could have just snapped his fingers and independently accomplished what he wanted to do. In no way did he *need* the woman's jars of olive oil or Moses' staff to achieve his plans, but he chose to use what they already had to perform the miraculous.

So what was in my hand? The treatment that the doctors were recommending to me was: the chemo, the immunotherapy, the surgery. Those were in my hand. *So God used those to bring about my healing.* It's hard to have gut wrenching faith when you've grown up in twenty-first-century America. We didn't see the Red Sea part or manna come from heaven or water burst forth from the rock. God knows that. Does that mean we should excuse ourselves from a life of trust? No. But it does mean that he gets it. No condemnation. Just the truth that I am a weenie. He knows it and I know it, and he still loves me. He will still heal me, and he will help me grow in my faith. Remember, it only takes a mustard seed to start.

Whatever limited amount of faith that I have does not diminish the power of God. For me, it only enhances his kindness. Even though I am lacking and unable to believe in him like I should (knowing he is all powerful God), he is still so merciful to me and works in the ways that I understand to bring about my well-being. What a kind Father!

When David went to face Goliath, why did he even bother to take the sling and a few stones? Why didn't he just march out, speak a word, and watch Goliath fall to the ground? Was David lacking faith because he decided to take along his well-known weapon of choice? That doesn't seem to be the case. He believed that God could and would take down Israel's enemy. He didn't know exactly how it was all going to pan out. He just knew that in the end, they'd have the victory. He took the only tools that he knew to take, and God used them to take down the largest foe of their day.

Can't it be the same now? What's in your hand? If you have the faith to speak to your situation and see that mountain move, I totally applaud you and hope that one day I will be there as well. I want to learn from you. Step by step. But if you are a weenie and aren't there yet, that does *not* mean you are excluded from seeing your giants fall. Use whatever God has put in your hand to witness your miracle.

Get in the Boat

Have you heard the anecdote about the man who was stuck on his rooftop during a flood? He fervently began to pray that God would save him. Soon after, someone in a row boat came by and shouted to the man, "I'm here to help you! Get in!" The man on the roof replied, "No thank you! I'm praying to God, and he is going to save me. I have faith." So the rowboat floated away.

Shortly after, someone in a motor boat saw the stranded man and approached him. "I'm here to help you! Get in!" the motorboat driver shouted. The man on the roof replied, "No thank you! I'm praying to God, and he is going to save me. I have faith." So the motorboat sped on.

Not too long after, a helicopter caught sight of the stranded man and the pilot shouted down to him, "I'm here to help you! Climb up this rope!" The man on the roof replied, "No thank you! I'm praying to God, and he is going to save me. I have faith." The pilot tried once more to rescue him but the man would not budge, so he reluctantly flew away.

Soon the water rose above the rooftop and the stranded man drowned. When he reached Heaven, he requested to speak with God and discuss the whole situation. As God approached him, the man exclaimed, "Why did you let me drown? I had faith that you were going to save me, but you didn't! I don't understand!" To this God replied, "I sent you a rowboat, a motorboat, and a helicopter. What more did you expect?"

Maybe I should have titled this book, *Faith for Dummies*. How often have I been like the man on the roof, praying for God to save me but not recognizing any of the vessels that he is sending? Once I prayed for patience, so God graciously allowed people into my life who rubbed me the wrong way. We all want the parade and fireworks. We all want the big show, the one that leaves us with no doubt that it was God. And every once in awhile, we do receive just that. But most of the time, the miracles occur right before our noses.

A friend shared with me the story of someone in her church who had badly injured his hand and was praying for healing. It was a long and slow process until he finally received what he had asked for. In complaint, he came to God and questioned him as to why he had never seen a healing occur. The Holy Spirit replied that he had, in fact, seen healing occur. The man was baffled. Surely he would remember such an event! When did he ever see that happen? God reminded him of the time he gashed his knee as a child. Was the wound still there? No, it had closed. And the time he injured his finger as a young man. Was the finger still painful? No, it had healed. God lovingly revealed to him that all of those healings were indeed from him. They were pre-built healings due to the way that God created our bodies to mend themselves.

The Bible says that every good and perfect gift is from the Father (James 1:17). Could I have been cured of cancer if I had never prayed one single prayer and didn't even believe in God? Absolutely. With the knowledge we currently possess in modern medicine, many people are healed without ever acknowledging God at all. And I am glad they are. God sends the rain to both the believer and the unbeliever. Who provided the wisdom to discover cures for cancer or any other ailment? God. Certainly the devil doesn't want people healed. I pray for God to supernaturally heal people of cancer but even more, I pray that he will release the knowledge needed to find a cure for it entirely.

Natural or Supernatural

I've heard a handful of Christians say that we should not seek medical help when we are sick, only pray. They believe that only sick people go to see the doctor, and if a person is in Christ then they can not technically be sick. That sounds interesting at first, but I disagree. People who want to get better also go to the doctor. And while it can be tempting to begin to let your illness define you, especially if it is a chronic illness, seeking medical attention is not in any way sinful or a sign of unbelief.

My husband and I heard a similar line of reasoning from some during the ten years that we lived on monthly support for our missionary work. If you are not familiar with this sort of way to earn a living, it went like this: churches and individuals gave finances monthly or as one-time donations to us so that we could continue the work of church planting and community development around the world. The organization that we worked for did not pay us a salary, but we (and many others) believed in the work that we did, so others supported us financially. There are many examples of this in Scripture as well, but I'll save that for another time.

"A missionary should only receive supernatural support directly from God," they would say. And then they would give an example of some missionary from hundreds of years ago who saw God supernaturally supply their needs. I have seen God supernaturally supply the needs of people as well. Money or supplies appearing at just the right time with no human explanation. It definitely happens. God still does it today, but to say that it is the *only* way to see God provide is nonsense and cannot be supported with the Bible.

I have come to believe that God's preference in providing for his people is to use *other people*! God can and does step in and provide supernaturally at times, but usually, he stirs up his Body to be generous. Why? *So that the givers can be just as blessed as the receivers!* Then the ones giving from the pews of the sending church can be just as involved in the work as the missionaries on the field. Because we are a Body, and when a body works, all of its parts are involved. God could do it all by himself, but he prefers to include us.

God could have constructed the ark by himself, but he asked Noah to build it. God could have sent angels to build his temple in 1 Kings, but he gifted and appointed skilled craftsmen to do the job. He could have come to earth as a fully grown human, but he chose the womb of a young, unknown woman to carry the Son of God. God likes to work with humans. God can and does perform miracles supernaturally, but he also uses doctors and medicine to cure us.

Every good and perfect gift is from him.

Prophetic, Not Pathetic

There is something in my vein of church tradition that we refer to as a "prophetic act." In other circles, it may be referred to as a step of faith, a symbolic action, a nudging from the Holy Spirit, or even a premonition (though I use that term carefully because it has other meanings). A prophetic act is basically an action that we take when we sense some sort of direction from God but have not yet seen it come to pass. We step out into the Spirit's "nudging" before we have seen in the physical what we've heard in the spiritual.

It's what I referred to in chapter four, when I sensed that the Lord wanted me to go and buy a toy for my third unborn baby-the one I carried after two miscarriages. It was an act of faith based on what I felt that God had spoken to me. I believed that he was saying that this baby would be born here on earth, and I needed to agree with his promise. So without any proof that this would come to pass other than what I sensed from God, I purchased a set of baby rattles from the local shop.

Is this crazy? Well, yes, to the person who doesn't believe in God. Is this Biblical? Yes! The Bible is full of examples of prophetic acts, though it doesn't label them as such. One well-known Bible story of a prophetic act is found in Joshua chapter six. The Israelites are on their way to take the Promised Land, but the walled city of Jericho stands before them. God tells Joshua that he has delivered Jericho into their hands, but nothing has physically happened yet. The wall is still strong, the city still intact, the soldiers still armed. God tells the Israelites to march around the city once a day for six days. On the seventh day, they are meant to march around the city seven times while the priests blow their trumpets. After the priests sound a long blast on their horns, everyone will shout and the walls will fall down.

How would you respond if God told you to do something similar? At this point, the people have absolutely no hint in the physical realm that this stronghold is going to fall. They only have a promise from God, but that promise is enough for them to move. They do as God instructs them to do. They march around the city six times, and on the seventh day, after marching seven times and hearing the trumpet blast, they all shout. And the great Wall of Jericho comes tumbling down. I doubt that it would have fallen if they had not listened to God and followed his instructions.

Another one of my favorite Biblical examples of a prophetic act can be found in 2 Kings 5. There is a great and valiant commander from the land of Aram named Naaman who has been infected with leprosy. There is no cure for him in all of

Aram, but he hears through a Hebrew slave girl about one of her prophets in Samaria who can heal him. The king of Aram sends a request on his behalf to the king of Israel, inquiring about this miracle prophet. The message eventually finds its way to the prophet Elisha who promises that God will do what he desires if Naaman comes to visit him.

Naaman arrives at Elisha's door with his entourage: servants and horses and chariots. Elisha sends a messenger to tell Naaman that his skin will be cleansed and restored if he goes down into the Jordan River and washes seven times. Naaman gets angry upon hearing this report. He wanted Elisha to come and wave his hands, and cure him from leprosy on the spot. He declares that the rivers of Damascus are just as good as the Jordan. What's so special about Israel's river that he needs to wash there? He's about to leave in a fit of rage when one of his incredibly wise servants approaches him and asks, "My father, if the prophet had told you to do some great thing, would you not have done it? How much more, then, when he tells you, 'Wash and be cleansed!'"

Naaman listens to the servant, humbles himself, and goes down to the Jordan. He dips in the water seven times like the man of God instructed him to do, and his skin is completely restored. The Bible says it "became clean like that of a young boy." Naaman is ecstatic and proclaims that there is no other God in all the world except in Israel.

Naaman receives instruction from God through the prophet Elisha, and without any physical evidence that what God says will come to pass, he humbles himself and obeys. God's word plus Naaman's faith-based action (or maybe just his hope-based action) opens the door to an incredible miracle.

Sometimes it can be easy to wish we had our personal prophet Elisha to give us clear and direct words from God. Well, the truth is that we have someone even better: the Holy Spirit! We don't have to travel all the way to Samaria to get a word from the Lord. We have the Spirit of God dwelling within us. No longer is God limited by a physical body, only speaking through prophets or restricted to one geographic location. He is now free to move about in the life of every believer who receives him. The Holy Spirit can initiate God's desires in our hearts. He can also confirm his word to us.

After Rich and I had spent over a decade living as missionaries in East Asia, we returned to the States and began working with a small missions agency based in the Carolinas. I loved living in that area, but that time in our lives was extremely stretching financially. We had two small children and an income that fell well below the federal poverty level. Although it was tight, we always had everything that we needed. God provided for us through many different avenues, but I remember our big splurge of the year was new bathroom towels! It was during this time that Rich and I both began to sense the Lord speaking to us about buying a home. In the physical realm, this seemed ridiculous, but years of walking with God had taught us that if he spoke it, he would somehow bring it to pass.

We began to look for homes in our area and applied for a loan. It was a seller's market and finding a decent home in our price point would most likely be a challenge. Actually, just qualifying for a loan with our type of non-traditional salary was going to be interesting. But the Lord led us to this cute little, two-story home on a cul-de-sac with a huge backyard, a pear tree, and a park down the hill and suggested that we try to buy it. It was a foreclosure that the bank had repossessed, flipped, and listed again on the market. Because of it's history, we were able to secure it at a price that we could afford. In fact, the appraisal came in $10,000 below the price that we had agreed to, but we got it anyway!

I still wonder at times how in the world a lender agreed to give us a loan, but God had said that he wanted to give us a home, so he lined it all up for us. I wish I could say that I followed him through that process without a care in the world, but I did not. There were more tears and more anxiety than necessary, but that didn't stop our Father from providing what he had promised.

This was a good gift that he wanted to give his children. It had always been a desire of my heart to have our own house, but I never considered that it would ever be a reality. Most of our adult lives up until that point had been spent in small, high-rise apartments in East Asia, always renting and never owning in case the government decided to kick us out for the work that we were doing. But our loving God wanted us to have a home of our own, so he initiated it, led us through the process, and made it happen. I'm so grateful to have such a kind Shepherd, one that gently leads each of his sheep to green pastures. Even the fearful, high-strung ones!

At that time, it didn't look like we had very much in our hands, but God doesn't require very much to work with. Think of the miracle that Jesus performed with just a few loaves of bread and two fish. He multiplied that small lunch to feed over five thousand people. God doesn't need a lot from you. All he asks is that you offer what you have to him in faith that he can use it to create something greater.

Chapter Nine

TRUSTING AGAIN AFTER DISAPPOINTMENT

"Far better is it to dare mighty things, to win glorious triumphs, even though checkered by failure... than to rank with those poor spirits who neither enjoy nor suffer much, because they live in a gray twilight that knows not victory nor defeat."

Theodore Roosevelt

When Faith Isn't Enough

I feel like it would not be fair to write a book about faith and not include what happens when we don't receive what we ask for. Because we are all going to have to experience that at one time or another. If we have not yet, then we will. We will never get it one hundred percent correct. And even if we do, there will be times that God doesn't do what we want him to do. What then?

151

The answer to our prayers does not rely on our own merit. In Psalm 115:1 it says, "Not to us but to your name be the glory." God does not differentiate between healing or not healing people based on their merit. None of us deserves anything from God. If you tell me that you wish you understood all of the ways of the Lord when it comes to healing and faith, I would reply, "Me too." I don't believe that we will ever fully understand until we meet with Jesus face to face. Until then, we live in the fog of this in-between world: not fully of this one yet not fully in the next.

My mother prayed and trusted for healing from cancer once in the 1980s, and she was healed. Again she prayed and trusted to be healed of cancer in 2010, but she did not receive what she asked for. Neither did we. Towards the end of her time on earth, when the cancer had moved into her brain and she was no longer fully with us, I would sit beside her bed every morning and read to her from her favorite devotion, *Streams in the Desert*. It's what I thought she might want me to do, and it brought me comfort as well.

"We have not passed this way heretofore, but the Lord Jesus has. It is all untrodden and unknown ground to us, but He knows it all by personal experience. The steep bits that take away our breath, the stony bits that make our feet ache so, the hot shadeless stretches that make us feel so exhausted, the rushing rivers that we have to pass through -- Jesus has gone through it all before us. 'He was wearied with his journey.' Not some, but all the many waters went over Him, and yet did not quench His love. He was made a perfect Leader by the things which He suffered. 'He knoweth our frame; he remembereth that we are dust.' Think of that when you are tempted to question the gentleness of His leading. He is remembering all

the time; and not one step will He make you take beyond what your foot is able to endure. Never mind if you think it will not be able for the step that seems to come next; either He will so strengthen it that it shall be able, or He will call a sudden halt, and you shall not have to take it at all."
Frances Ridley Havergal *(Streams in the Desert)*

I still continued to pray for healing but was losing hope. One day, I finally asked God if I should keep praying for healing or not. Immediately I received two pictures in my mind, one right after another. They might sound a bit silly to you, but they were deeply personal and meaningful to me, and I knew exactly what God meant by them.

Remembering that my mother was raised on a farm in Iowa which is known for its corn, the first picture that I received was that of corn stalk. The head of corn was coming out of the husk. The second picture was that of a caterpillar becoming a butterfly, one of my mother's favorite creatures. I recognized in my spirit that both pictures meant that she was leaving this body and receiving her new one. The caterpillar finding its new eternal beauty and the uncovered corn revealed in its truest form of glory. I began to weep, knowing that it was time to stop praying for healing and begin to ask God to take her Home. How would I live without her?

Two months after her passing, our baby girl was born. When I was pregnant with her, Rich and I tossed around a few names in preparation of her arrival, but it wasn't until the Holy Spirit whispered a name into my heart that we settled on one. It happened one day mid-pregnancy when I was praying for her. The image of a pearl came to mind. I thought that maybe it represented some kind of characteristic which she would possess, but as the months passed, the same image returned. I sensed that her name should be Pearl. She was seven months in the womb when her grandmother went to Heaven, and it was at that point when I fully understood the impact of her name.

A natural pearl forms when an oyster intercepts some kind of irritant inside of its shell. To defend itself, it forms a fluid around the invader. Layer upon layer is added until the pearl is formed.[13] This beautiful gem exists only because something painful preceded it. In the painful months that followed my mom's death, our daughter Pearl brought comfort and hope to everyone in our family and especially to me. God had brought beauty in the midst of our suffering.

We do not always receive what we want, even if we have faith that can move mountains. Hebrews 11, the most well-known chapter in the Bible on faith, discusses this exact point:

"And what more shall I say? I do not have time to tell about Gideon, Barak, Samson and Jephthah, about David and Samuel and the prophets, who through faith conquered kingdoms, administered justice, and gained what was promised; who shut the mouth of lions, quenched the fury of the flames, and escaped the edge of the sword; whose weakness was turned to strength; and who became powerful in battle and routed foreign armies. Women received back their dead, raised to life again. There were others who were tortured, refusing to be released so that they might gain an even better resurrection. **Some faced jeers and flogging, and even chains and imprisonment. They were put to death by stoning; they were sawed in two; they were killed by the sword. They went about in sheepskins and goatskins, destitute, persecuted and mistreated- the world was not worthy of them. They wandered in deserts and mountains,**

living in caves and holes in the ground. These were all
commended for their faith, yet none of them received what
had been promised, since God had planned something better
for us so that only together with us would
they be made perfect."
Hebrews 11:32-40

The world was not worthy of them. I have seen people who
have much greater faith than I not receive what they asked of
God. At some point in time, we all must die. Not one of us will
live forever. It is said that Smith Wigglesworth, the plumber
turned "Apostle of Faith" in the 1800s, brought his wife back
from the dead multiple times until she finally told him to let her
go. Wigglesworth clearly had the faith intact to perform the
miracle but had to agree with her that it was indeed time for her
to go home to be with the Lord.

I have heard some pastors share that we either receive our
healing down here on earth or our ultimate healing up in
Heaven. I never really liked hearing those words. I know it's
meant to be comforting, but it always sounded a little bit trite to
me. A way to excuse God when he doesn't give us what we
want. Or a way to excuse ourselves if we give up and let go of
God's promises. But that does not deny the fact that it is still
true. Death no longer has any sting for followers of Jesus. If we
don't receive what we want down here, we will get it in Heaven
and more. So much more.

Poor Job

How can you really have a chapter about disappointment and
suffering without mentioning Job? It would be a cowardly

avoidance. The book of Job has caused much theological heart wrenching over the years. And honestly, a lot of what comes out of Christians' mouths today still sounds like the explanations Job's friends were giving thousands of years ago, but there is an element of great comfort in the book as well.

I've heard and read many commentaries about Job. Some say that Job was on trial. Others say that God was actually on trial and Job was the judge: is God good or not? Some say that Job was a foreshadowing of Jesus. Others say that Job was the self-righteous one, thus deserving of the suffering because he did not repent and continued to accuse God. Some point out that God did not bring about Job's pain but Satan did; God only allowed it. Others say that Job's suffering allowed mercy to be poured out onto Abraham, who would follow him chronologically in the story of God's people. Some of these views I find interesting. Others I do not, but one aspect is certain: it's easy to hypothesize about suffering until you actually walk through it yourself.

The Book of Job is raw. Amongst other ideas, it is a naked account of one follower of God walking through great turmoil and anguish. He asks all the questions. He despairs all the despairs. He loses everything he has, save his own life. The advice of his friends is of no comfort to him. He cries out for God to answer but there is only silence until the very end of the book. That is when God shows up.

In the last few chapters of Job, God speaks. Not in the way that Job had planned, but exactly in the way that Job needed:

> *"Where were you when I laid the earth's foundation?*
> *Tell me, if you understand.*

Who marked off its dimension? Surely you know!
Who stretched a measuring line across it?
On what were its footings set,
or who laid its cornerstone-
while the morning stars sang together
and all the angels shouted for joy?

Who shut up the sea behind doors
when it burst forth from the womb,
when I made the clouds its garment
and wrapped it in thick darkness,
when I fixed limits for it
and set its doors and bards in place,
when I said, "This far you may come and no farther;
here is where your proud waves halt"?

Have you ever given orders to the morning,
or shown the dawn its place,
that it might take the earth by the edges
and shake the wicked out of it?"
Job 38:4-13

God continues on like this for a good four chapters, revealing his wisdom and power, his greatness and sovereignty to Job. Job's circumstances have not changed at all, and not one of his questions has been answered, but at the end of God's monologue, this is Job's response:

"' I know that you can do all things;
no purpose of yours can be thwarted.
You asked, "Who is this that obscures
my plans without knowledge?"

Surely I spoke of things I did not understand,
things too wonderful for me to know.

'You said, "Listen now, and I will speak;
I will question you,
and you shall answer me,"

My ears had heard of you
but now my eyes have seen you.
Therefore I despise myself
and repent in dust and ashes.'"
Job 42:2-6

At the end of the story, God restores to Job twice as much as he lost. The latter part of his life was more blessed than the first part (and the first part was already very blessed). But God never gives an explanation for the suffering. He never tells Job why he allowed Satan to capsize his life. He only opens Job's eyes to see a glimpse of his greatness. And that was enough for Job.

So I no longer read commentaries on Job because I think that's the point: there will always be some amount of mystery in the path of suffering. I don't believe we will ever fully understand it on this side of Heaven. I wonder if we were even meant to. There will most likely always be something of a question mark. God himself doesn't even answer the questions posed to him in his own book.

When you are walking through grief and suffering yourself, all the commentaries and theological answers in the world will not take your pain away. Only catching sight of God's glory can do that. Only a revelation of his power and his goodness, an understanding that he is still in charge no matter what happens to us here. He can *and he will* work everything out for our good. This is the answer that we truly need. And it's the only answer that brings peace in the storm and quiets our souls. He is enough. Him alone.

Promise of What's to Come

Mixed in with all of the devastating sadness and grief that accompanied me after my mother's death was an overwhelming sense of gratitude to Jesus for paying the price that guaranteed me a chance to see my mom again one day. One day, when this world is done and all is made new. One day, when all is made right.

Our area of Colorado is not particularly known for rainbows because we receive very little rain. I never saw even one near my home in all the years that we lived there. But just hours after my mother had gone to be with Jesus, a huge colorful arc appeared right over the ten acres that belonged to my parents. It was my mom's way of saying that she was home, not to worry. All was well. In fact, there were so many rainbows that day in Durango that the newspaper even wrote an article about the phenomenon the next day in the town's paper. Well done, good and faithful servant.

"Good people pass away; the godly often die before their time. But no one seems to care or wonder why. No one seems to understand that God is protecting them from the evil to come. For those who follow godly paths will rest in peace when they die."
Isaiah 57:1-2

I stumbled upon this verse in the days following my mom's passing, and it brought me comfort. In the years that came after her death, there were various reasons for heartache within our family. I wonder sometimes if God just decided that she'd seen enough. Or maybe she decided it herself. I don't know.

A friend wrote to me shortly after I was diagnosed with cancer myself and wondered if I longed for my mother during this difficult time even more than on any other given day. And though of course I always want her to be here with us, in one way I was glad that she no longer was. The only thing worse than walking through a cancer diagnosis and subsequent treatment yourself is watching your child do it. I was happy that she was spared that agony. You could say that God protected her from that evil. Even though she would have rather been beside me to help me, she didn't have to carry that burden. And for that, I am grateful.

The truth is that we were not made for pain. We were made for a garden. We were made for unbroken relationship with our Creator and with others. We were made for a perfect world. Clearly this earth's present state is not the direction that God hoped humanity would take when he formed us. C.S. Lewis so eloquently describes it:

"If we find ourselves with a desire that nothing in this world can satisfy, the most probable explanation is that we were made for another world."

This desire is like the robin of spring that appears in the dead of winter. A harbinger of what lies ahead. If we didn't know any better, we would assume that the bird must have lost its way, carried into our frozen land by some brutal storm. But the robin knows what's coming. And because of the consistency of the changing seasons, so do we. He may seem a little ahead of his time, but the song in his breast brings comfort and reminds us that winter will not last forever. New life is on its way.

Made for Comfort

As humans, we must have this comfort. We *must* have it. This type of comfort is a solace, a consolation from the pain and disappointment that we *will* experience in this life. If we don't learn how to receive comfort from God, we will find it in other sources, for we cannot live without it. Without God, we will find comfort in addictions of various kinds: technology, food, alcohol, relationships, sex, drugs, busyness, social media but none of these things will bring the healing that we so desperately need.

When wondering how to live in wholeness as a human, I look to Jesus, the perfect one. The Bible says that he was a man of sorrows and acquainted with grief (Isaiah 53:3). He was fully God yet fully man. He experienced all of the disappointments and doubts that we did, yet he did not succumb to them. He knew how to stay close to his Father in the lowest valleys of life. Let's look at some of ways that Jesus responded to pain and grief:

1) Jesus doesn't trivialize the pain.

Jesus doesn't minimize the anguish or try to brush it away. He feels it. He allows himself to be overcome with the emotion that pain produces. We see Jesus at the tomb of his good friend, Lazarus, in John 11, weeping because he had died. Even though he knew that he was going to bring Lazarus back to life in just a matter of minutes, Jesus doesn't jump ahead too soon to what will come. He just stays in the grief for a moment and allows space for it. This world is not as it should be. That is sad. We can acknowledge those feelings too.

2) Jesus expresses his grief.

Jesus expressed his emotions. He wept when he was sad. He laughed when he was happy. He told the disciples when he felt disappointed or was frustrated with their actions. And when he was mad, he flipped over some tables. The point is that Jesus knew that the proper response to emotions was to *feel* them and express them in a healthy way, so he did just that.

After my mom passed away, I received a phone call from one of the hospice nurses. She was checking in on us to make sure we were doing okay. I briefly summed up how things were going and she offered me a very helpful bit of advice that I have held onto since. She said that our own souls know what we need to do to grieve, so we should listen to them.

Everyone grieves in their own way. We are not to judge how another grieves or compare ourselves with them. Some people grieve by withdrawing to be alone, and others grieve by making a tribute or memorial to the deceased. Some grieve by feeling and others by doing, and most usually do a little of both.

I listened the woman's advice and took time to feel the emotions in the days that followed the funeral. And also in the years that followed those days. I had a bracelet inscribed with my mom's handwriting and two stuffed bears made out of her clothes for my children. I put together a quilt with her shirts and set a memorial stone in the garden. I watched slideshows of her pictures and listened to songs that reminded me of her when I missed her. I took walks in nature. I wrote her letters.

There is a time for everything. We would be wise to recognize the need to grieve large and small occurrences in our lives. This allows us to heal and eventually move past the initial pain.

3) Jesus withdraws to spend time with his Father.

Over and over, we see Jesus taking time alone to be with his Father. After his cousin John is beheaded, after long days of ministry, and before the biggest challenge of his life, we see Jesus by himself, pouring his heart out to his dad.

There is a comfort that resides in the heart of God that we as humans cannot find in any other place. There is no friend or family member, no parent or spouse who can comfort us the way that the Spirit of God can. *No one.* Only he knows the intricate weavings of our inner beings. Only he can fill those voids with his love and mercy. We must pull away during difficult times to share our hearts with him and hear his heart towards us.

4) Jesus hears the Father's affirmations.

Before his big test in the wilderness, the one where he would fast for forty days and forty nights and the devil would come and tempt him to disobey God, Jesus hears the encouragement that he needs from his Father in Matthew 3:17, "This is my beloved son, in who I am well-pleased."

It's so much easier to walk through a trial when we know that God is walking with us. When we believe that he is for us and not against us, then we know that we are not on our own and he is not out to get us. That knowledge allows us to lean into God instead of turning away from him when we face difficult times. Jesus knew this and heard it again before a long and challenging stint in the wilderness. Perhaps it helped to carry him through.

5) Jesus uses God's Word to resist temptation.

When doubt and accusation tried to trip Jesus up as he wandered in the desert, Jesus stood on God's Word and kept the enemy at bay. In Matthew 4, we read how Satan came to him with three different tests. The first questioned Jesus' identity. The second questioned God's care and ability to protect Jesus. And the third was the promise of prestige, money, and control in exchange for his soul. Sounds similar to the questions posed in the Garden. We should expect no different in our own lives, so we need to know how Jesus withstood them.

Jesus used God's Word every time the enemy came at him. "It is written..." he quoted the Scriptures each time. It's the same for us. When the enemy comes at us with fears and doubts, accusations about God or ourselves, we need to have some kind of weapon to get him off our back. The Word of God is our sword (Ephesians 6).

If we resist the devil, he will flee (James 4:7). We must go back to the words that God has given us. If we don't know of any yet, then we need to get into the Bible and find some. Ask the Holy Spirit to lead you to promises that you can stand on when the arrows of the enemy come at you.

6) Jesus honors the good.

Just after John the Baptist, Jesus' cousin, is jailed in Matthew 11, John sends his disciples to ask Jesus if he really is the Messiah. Jesus doesn't rebuke John for his questions. Instead he points John's disciples to the miracles themselves as proof that he is who he says he is. I wonder if Jesus knows that the imminent death of his friend is just ahead because as John's disciples turn to go (but are still within hearing distance), Jesus begins to speak to the crowd about how awesome John is: solid, a prophet, committed, no one greater.

This life is short and passes quickly, so we must take time to honor those around us while we have them and also after we lose them. In the midst of life's disappointments, when we take time to recall the good, our hearts are again lifted.

7) Jesus leans on his close friends.

Just before Jesus goes to the cross, he asks his three closest friends to come away with him and pray. They of course fall asleep, but Jesus has invited them into this time of excruciating turmoil. In the mess of emotion and fear of the future, Jesus allows others to be close to him. Too often we only want others near us when life looks good. After the storm has passed, we may reach out a close friend or two and share what's been going on but to do so *in the midst* of the crazy requires real vulnerability. Jesus asks his friends to stand with him while the storm is raging. He knows that he is made for connection, so he invites others into his pain even though they don't respond to it perfectly.

8) Jesus receives help from others.

Jesus' life was a ministry to others, but he received ministry as well. We see how Jesus accepts hospitality from various families and individuals (Luke 19), how he lives off of the support of some generous women (Luke 8:1-3), and how the woman pours perfume on his feet and prepares him for his burial (Matthew 26). All of these people ministered to Jesus, and he received it.

It is sometimes easier to *give* encouragement, money, and help to those around us than it is to receive it for ourselves. This is sometimes just due to pride. As humans, we need each other. We will all face challenges at one time or another. We need to be able to sit on the receiving end as well as the giving one.

When I was sick, I said yes to many meals, gift cards, house-cleanings, and babysitting. I needed help because I am human and cannot do it all on my own. My family needed help and God provided his Body, his hands and feet, to do the job. I am forever grateful. And guess what? Those generous souls were blessed in return for their giving because Jesus promised that whatever we do for the least of these, we've done for him. And we'll be rewarded (Matthew 25).

9) Jesus surrenders.

Jesus didn't want to go to the cross. I mean, he did but he didn't. He willingly made a choice to go to the cross (John 10:18), but he did not want to experience the pain of what the cross meant. We see this torment as he asks his Father to please "take this cup from him," in Luke 22:42. But Jesus knows that the way to freedom is always through surrender. He trusts the Father even though he doesn't humanly want to walk the path that has been set before him and later says in that same passage, "Not my will but yours be done."

10) Jesus looks towards the coming joy.

Jesus was willing to walk through one of the most excruciating deaths known to man because of the joy that was set before him (Hebrews 12:2). He kept his heart focused on the reward that was to come: humanity in restored relationship to God. With that in mind, he set his face like flint. There was a purpose to the suffering.

We don't always understand the "why" behind our pain, and I don't think all of it has as divine a consequence as Jesus' did, but God has promised to use everything that we have to walk through for good (Romans 8:28). We can be sure of that. God's plan is always one of restoration. No matter what is lost, God's purposes are always to give you more than what has been taken. His plans are for you and not against you (Jeremiah 29:11).

Our God is a God of suffering (Isaiah 53:4). He is also a God of comfort (2 Corinthians 1:3-5). When we journey through the valley of the shadow of death, we must lean into him until we receive what we need. Whether it be through a verse, a song, the listening ear of a friend, a gift card, or his presence resting upon us, he will come. He longs to show us mercy even more than we want to receive it.

Just today I had to go in for a CT scan of my brain because I have been having some unexplained dizziness. It's possible that it's just sinus pressure, but of course everyone's minds jump to a brain tumor. And that's a realistic possibility, so they had me checked just to be sure. My doctor called a few hours later to tell me that the scan was normal. I thanked her, hung up the phone, sat down on my kitchen floor, and let big tears of relief roll down my cheeks.

I sometimes long for the days of my youth, before I knew what loss and death and fear really meant. But for those of us who have lived in the shadows of sickness and pain, we must relearn what it is to walk again in the light of God's goodness.

The only real and lasting peace that I can find when I think about all the fears of the unknown future is in the promise that

God will be there too. In fact, he already is in all of our tomorrows, for he is not limited by time. He will give me the grace and wisdom to walk through whatever this life will bring, and that gives me the confidence to continue on down this journey. My hero Corrie Ten Boom (again) says this:

"Never be afraid to trust an unknown future to a known God."

He is the only one that I am sure of. We are not guaranteed a life without pain. In fact, we are guaranteed to have trouble. But Jesus already overcame it and can lead us through to victory even after disappointment.

"Return to your fortress, you prisoners of hope; even now I announce that I will restore twice as much to you."
Zechariah 9:12

Chapter Ten

THE TENACITY OF FAITH

"Yeah, I know that there is pain
But you hold on for one more day and you
Break free, break from the chains."

Wilson Phillips

When You're Going Through Hell, Keep Going!

There was a picture that was popular about ten years ago before we actually called these kinds of pictures memes. It was the one with a stork trying to eat a frog. Maybe you saw it? The frog is already inside of the stork's bill, but the frog hands are around the stork's neck in attempts to strangle him. The frog is not letting go until that stork releases him! That is my visual of tenacious faith. And faith does often feel like that: like there's no way that this could turn out as God promised, but if he said it, I believe it, so I'm going to keep holding on! My responsibility is to not let go. His responsibility is to perform the miracle.

Jesus tells a tale in Luke 18 about a widow who needed justice against her adversary. The judge in her town was unjust, didn't fear God or care about what people thought and didn't have time to help her. But she persisted. She continued to come and demand justice. She would not give up. And because she did not let go, the judge finally conceded and gave her what she asked for. Jesus compares this unjust judge to God- if even a man like this would give justice to the needy, how much more will God? Jesus also asks, "But will he find faith on the earth?"

That question has stuck with me over the years. Will Jesus find faith on the earth when he returns? Does he find it now? Does he find it in me? My prayer is that he always will. What kind of faith is he looking for? The answer is in the story that he told in conjunction with the question, in the life of the persistent widow. She never gave up hope that her request would be answered, even though she was asking a cruel man. She never lost heart.

This is not an emotional faith. This is a faith that banks everything on the goodness of God. This kind of faith is convinced that he will come through because he said he would, so it keeps showing up, waiting for the expected promise to be realized. Because God has spoken it, this faith has eyes open to see the hope fulfilled.

This type of faith-ask is different than simply begging God to do something. If we understand God's disposition as a father, we know that we do not have to beg. We do not have to try to convince him to help us or plead for him to intervene. He's not sitting up in Heaven with his arms crossed, annoyed that we are once again in need of help. The way that we approach our Father is not like a Buddhist prayer wheel where the answer to our request comes only if we can manage to turn the wheel thousands of times.

Hebrews 4:16 tells us that we can "confidently approach the throne of grace so that we may receive mercy and find grace to help us in our time of need." We can assuredly present our requests to God and leave it in his hands. This type of prayer is not based in fear that God has not heard or will not give us what we request if we don't ask again and again. If our request is according to his will, then we can trust that it's on its way. He wants it more than we do. This type of prayer is a faith-ask, a victory-ask. It's a "please can I have this, thank-you that it's coming" ask. Thank you that it's here. Thank you that it's done. Can't wait to see it!

The way we perceive God as we present our requests to him is foundational, but so is the way that we perceive ourselves. Do we view ourselves as worthy of his help? Do we think we deserve it? Are we lacking in some way? If the focus is on us, we will always come up short. Sure, sometimes we are in the way of what God wants for us, what is best for us, and in his kindness he does not grant every request that we make (thank-you, God for not letting me marry my high-school boyfriend!) He does this not because he is stingy, *but because he is wise and good.*

The truth is that God longs to show us mercy. He's leans toward mercy. He wants mercy more than justice. We don't *deserve* healing or salvation or favor or grace. Time and time again, we prove that we put ourselves at the center of the world and want it to rotate around us. But we are his children, and he is a good father who gives good gifts to his kids. If accusing thoughts come to say that we do not deserve whatever we are asking for-make it easy and agree. It's the truth! We don't deserve it! But Jesus does. Jesus made us worthy. God loved us in our own selfishness. In our own sin, he gave his life for us. There's not greater love. His favor and help is not dependent upon us, it's dependent upon him. He is good. He is loving. He is merciful. He is faithful. Even when we're not. That is the solid truth.

We don't need to beg him to help. He's already on it. He knows what we need before we even ask (Matthew 6:8). He's just longing for us to call out. He's hoping that we continue to stick it out even when the answer seems delayed or doesn't come as we expected. He sees and knows the masterpiece that he is in the process of making, even when we only see stage one. He sees our full potential.

I've always found the passage in Daniel 10 intriguing. Daniel has been praying and fasting, crying out to God for an answer over his nation Israel. After many days, an angel finally appears and tells Daniel that *since the first day that he asked,* his words were heard, and that he, the angel has come in response to them. In fact, the reason that the angel was delayed was due to spiritual warfare in the heavenly realms. Wowza!

We do not always know what is going on behind the scenes of our prayers. Actually, we seldom do, but we can be sure that God longs to intervene. He is the deliverer. That's what he does. If we hold on for his answer, he will show up in his fullness and radiance. It will blow us away, and we will love him even more.

I believe we must learn more of this thank-ask. We ask. We believe he hears. We don't see it yet, but we know the answer is coming. We trust. We continue to thank him for what he is going to do. We praise him for the good that he will bring about. We continue to thank him even as we ask to see it come to pass. The thank-ask. Even if we're being swallowed by a stork, we try with everything we've got to strangle that stork and hold on for God's deliverance.

God Will Bring it to Pass

In the Book of Genesis, we find the story of a man named Joseph. Jospeh has a dream (a literal one) that one day his family will all bow down to him. He believes that he's going to be a boss even though he's the second to youngest in the family of a very patriarchal society. Chances were slim in the natural, but God gave him a new reality when he wrote that dream into his heart.

Fast forward a few years and we don't see Joseph ruling over anything. We see his brothers selling him as a slave to Egypt. We see him accused and imprisoned. Very unremarkable. It looks as though God has forgotten Joseph and the dream was just a fluke. But Joseph does not give up on God. He continues to serve him and do his best no matter what situation he finds himself in. And in the end, due to a change of events that Joseph never could have manipulated on his own, Joseph was put in charge of not just his family but all of Egypt. Joseph's faithfulness saved the space for God to prove his word true.

Joseph remained faithful with whatever was put in front of him. Faithful with his slave duties. Faithful with his prison responsibilities. And eventually faithful with the most powerful nation in the world. God does not overlook anything.

How easy it would have been for Joseph to accuse God in the middle of his story. How easy it would have been for bitterness and resentment to actually prevent Joseph from receiving what God wanted to give him. We must resist the temptation to judge the ending of our stories when they are only half-written.

Before I was even diagnosed with cancer, just days after I had felt a lump, the Holy Spirit told me that he was going to part the Red Sea for me and that he would get glory. (I should have known at that moment that the lump was not benign.) Once the diagnosis came, the storm began to pound, but I held onto the rock of God's word. He had promised that he was going to bring me through, and I believed him. I clearly could not heal myself. I prayed for supernatural healing, but it did not come. I went through rounds of chemo and radiation and immunotherapy and trusted that God would not let me be consumed. I would never have been able to do that in my own strength. It was God's word that saw me through. By trusting in the promise of God, I was able to see my mountain moved.

Walking by faith means having the end vision in sight. We must recall what God said would happen. We know the *big* ending- that one day Jesus will return and all will be made right, a new heaven and earth, kingdom come, big picture stuff. We must learn to live with this eternity in our hearts, but we must also receive his word, his promises for the storms along our path *in this life*. Then we are able to stand when we have nothing else to cling to. If we lose a job or a friend or a home or a loved one, the word of God will bring comfort and help and strength in those times of need.

When I read of the people in the Bible who saw the power of God in their lives, I see a certain tenacity in them. It's an almost offensive boldness. They will not take no for an answer. They are holding on, pit-bulling it, until they get what they ask for. They put all their eggs in the basket of God's goodness and almost, if you will, *demand* to the universe that what they have been promised comes to pass. They have banked everything on the hope that God will come through, and in fact, Jesus *commends* this type of faith.

There is a story of a Gentile woman who asks Jesus to heal her daughter in Matthew 15. Jesus' first response seems to brush her off. He tells her that he came only to help the Jewish people, not Gentiles such as herself. But she persists. She is humble and desperate enough to refuse to play by the religious rules. She needs help, and she knows Jesus can help her, so she asks again, begging for even the crumbs that the dogs drop on the floor, alluding to the leftovers of healing and help reserved for Gentiles after the Jews had their fill. At this point Jesus stops, praises the greatness of her faith, and grants her request, healing her daughter.

If we fail to realize what Jesus is doing, his response to the woman feels cold and harsh. But he is actually calling out the tenacious faith he sees within her. "Why should I take the children's bread and give it to the dogs?" Jesus asks. "But even the dogs get crumbs," she replies. Breathtaking.

Faith vs Fatalism

Far too often we give up before the answer comes because we agree with the lie that God will not come through for us. Faith is vulnerable. What if he doesn't come through? What if he holds out on us? What if my fear comes to pass? But to live without faith is fatalism.

Fatalism is defined as "the belief that all events are predetermined and therefore inevitable" or "a submissive outlook, resulting in a fatalistic attitude." Fatalism submits to what's at hand. Circumstances are bad? Oh well, nothing I can do about it. It is, in fact, in direct opposition to how God intends for us to live. The command that he gave to "multiply and tend to the earth" is the *opposite* of fatalism. It is the opposite of submission to whatever comes at us. God desires forward motion and forward motion is NOT PASSIVE. It must be active. Fatalism is usually a learned way of living, but it can rob us of all that God has in store.

Millions of people in the world live their lives through a fatalistic filter. Entire cultural worldviews are founded upon it. Take for instance the caste system, most notable in India where traditionally if one is born into a low caste, nothing he does can ever lift him out of that fate. We can live our lives in the same manner. Giving up hope that a family member will ever come back to God. Succumbing to a tolerable marriage. Resigning ourselves to a mediocre job or overwhelming debt because it's too tiring to hope and work for better. And it is tiring. Hope can be a tiring task. To raise one's heart up again and again can be draining at times, but raise it we must.

Fatalism defies faith. Faith resists the idea that we have no power to change our circumstances. Faith reminds us that we can do all things because Jesus is strengthening us. It's impossible to read the Bible and NOT see how people of faith changed the world by taking hold of God's word and walking it out *with* Him. God does not intend for us to just go with the flow like a limp twig in the river. We are rocks, made in his image, resisting when evil occurs and bringing his kingdom with us wherever we go. To our jobs, to our families, to our bodies, to our world. Is it easy? By all means, no. But the Bible says in Matthew 11:12 that the righteous must take it by force.

If we circle back again to the Israelites' unwillingness to take the Promised Land because it involved a fight, we can see all that they missed out on in that generation. And even when their children grew and invaded the occupied territory, they still allowed so much evil in the land instead of battling as they should have. Far too often, I live in the same manner.

We must recall the ways that God has come through for us in the past. Remind our own hearts that he is faithful and he will continue to be. Speak the truths of God found throughout the Bible that inspire our souls to take courage once again. We must ask God for the encouragement that we need to strengthen ourselves and give us the spiritual sustenance required to continue the journey.

The story of the woman in 2 Kings 4 is so inspiring to me. This is the woman who asks her husband to build a little room on the roof of their home for the prophet Elisha to stay in when he passes through their area. She recognizes him as a prophet and wants to show him hospitality. He in turn asks what he can do to repay their kindness. She requests nothing, but he notices that she is childless and promises her that God will give her a son in a year's time. Sure enough, God's word, spoken through the prophet comes to pass.

The child grows and one day finds himself out in the fields helping his father when he is overtaken by a headache. He is carried back to the house for his mother to tend. Within hours, it seems, the boy dies. His mother lays him on the bed in the prophet's rooftop room and sends for a horse and carriage to take her to see Elisha.

Elisha's servant, Gehazi sees her coming from a distance and goes to meet her, asking what is wrong. She discloses nothing and presses onto see Elisha. The woman throws herself at the prophet's feet, but God does not reveal to him what has happened. She must tell him.

Elisha tells her that Gehazi will go ahead and help the boy, but the woman will not accept that answer. She swears to God that she will not leave unless Elisha personally comes home with her. He concedes, goes to the woman's house to see about the boy, and the boy is eventually healed in dramatic detail.

This woman is tenacious. She is past niceties and manners and does not accept the prophet's "no". He would have been a highly honored man in her culture with much authority, but she does not allow fear or protocol to stop her. She is over it. She wants her son healed, and she's not content with just the servant. She's waiting for the real deal. She's not leaving until she gets it. So guess what? *She gets it.*

Sometimes we have to take the risk and press through the red tape, the religious rules that want to keep us in place, the polite "should do's" that can hold us back from seeing the breakthrough that God intends for us. We have to be ruthless with fatalism and stand guard against thoughts that tell us it will always be like this, that this is just the way life goes, and nothing will ever change. Yes, life is hard and we cannot avoid all hardship, but there is always hope. We are not doomed to live in a place where the glass remains in a permanently half-empty state. God doesn't half-bake anything. What he begins, he will see to completion.

> *"'Shall I bring to the time of birth and*
> *not cause delivery?' says the Lord.*
> *'Shall I who cause delivery shut up*
> *the womb?' says your God."*
> Isaiah 66:9

What do you need Jesus to do for you? Do you continue to believe and ask for it, or have you resigned yourself to live life without it? It can be tiring, the continual ask. It sometimes seems easier to disconnect from the real desires that we have and live in the grayness of daily life. I wonder if that is why Jesus asked the crippled man if he *wanted* to be healed?

The story is in John 5. There is a pool in Jerusalem which is known to be a place where those who are lame, blind, paralyzed, or invalid come and wait to be healed. Jesus sees a crippled man who has been ill for 38 years. He knew that man had been lying there for a very long time, but instead of automatically healing the man, he asks him, "Do you want to be healed?" Um, Jesus that's awkward. Not very politically correct of you, Lord. *Do you want to be healed?* The answer seems fairly obvious, but the question must have been needed or Jesus would not have asked it. He never over speaks.

It is the same question that Jesus asks us today. Do you want to be healed? Do you want to be made well? Are you comfortable with the pain? Have you accustomed yourself to living like you do? It doesn't have to be this way.

When Jesus asks the man this question, he replies by telling Jesus why he has not yet been healed. Jesus responds to him with a command, "Get up and walk." The reasons why it hasn't worked before don't matter any longer. If Jesus is on the scene, our lives will change. Healing is possible. Healed relationships are possible. A changed heart is possible. It's all possible with him. The question is if we want it or not.

A couple of years ago, Rich and I were celebrating our ten-year anniversary. We'd had a pretty good decade of life together. Nothing major to complain about. But I suppose I had assumed that after ten years of marriage, I wouldn't react to the small annoyances in the same way that I responded as a newlywed. I figured I would have outgrown some of those bad habits by then. But I hadn't. We still got into the rut of arguing with each other in times of frustration.

Even though it was toned down a bit from the early years, I really hadn't matured all that much. It would have been easier to just let it go. Our marriage was good enough. But something inside whispered that there could be more. So we opted for marriage counseling through a local church. We watched the videos and did the workbook. I can't say that there was anything mind-blowing about it all, but it was the effort and time we took to put into it, the silent prayer that God would grow us more into his image, as a couple.

We're still a work in progress, but I don't ever want to come to a place of accepting mediocrity. If there is more, I would like to have it. I would like to have what Jesus says is possible. Some days, I'm too tired to even think about it, but on the good days, I still hope for what he dreams of when he sees my life, my marriage, my family. I don't want to settle for what is now. I want to have what could be. Often that simply looks like taking the next step that's in front of you until you've arrived where you want to be.

Tenacious faith can simply mean showing up again tomorrow, and trying again when it seems hopeless. It can be leaving the lights on when there hasn't been anyone wandering home in years. Sometimes it just means doing the next right thing until God moves. Faith doesn't always look glamorous. Hanging onto God's word until he brings it about is often a dirty job, but if we don't give up, we too can receive what is promised.

Even the weeniest amongst us.

ACKNOWLEDGEMENTS

I want to first acknowledge Jesus. Without him, I would not be where I am today. He paid the price in his own body for me to be free spiritually as well as physically. If I could live a thousand lifetimes, I would never be able to repay him for all he has given me.

I also want to acknowledge my friends and family who encouraged me to write this book and those who took the time to read, edit, and build it along the way. This has been a labor of love. Thank you.

Thank you to my most precious family who endured many mac and cheese dinners and an unkempt home so that I could put this together. I love you.

And thank you to my mother, who taught me that the strongest faith us not usually the flashiest. In the mundane chores of life, it is proven true.

ABOUT THE AUTHOR

Brooke Grangard is a Bible teacher, author, and Christian speaker. She is an ordained minister and founder of the non-profit Mobiles for Missions. Brooke spent a decade of her life serving as a missionary in East Asia where she met her husband and they grew to be a family of four.

Brooke has learned from walking through some of life's toughest valleys (fighting cancer, losing loved ones, and pregnancy loss) that God remains faithful in life's storms even when we don't. She now has a passion to share this message of hope and encouragement with others. She currently lives and ministers in Colorado and online at brookegrangard.com.

Notes

[1] http://ati.iblp.org/ati/family/articles/concepts/rhema/

[2] http://www.everystudent.com/features/bible.html

[3] John 1

[4] John 6:35

[5] Psalm 25:14

[6] Matthew 4:1

[7] Romans 1:20

[8] https://worldchallenge.org/devotion/acting-fear

[9] https://www.psychologytoday.com/us/blog/envy/201902/loneliness-new-epidemic-in-the-usa

[10] https://www.tandfonline.com/doi/abs/10.1080/10503307.2016.1169332?scroll=top&needAccess=true&journalCode=tpsr20

[11] https://greatergood.berkeley.edu/article/item/how_gratitude_changes_you_and_your_brain

[12] https://www.connectsavannah.com/savannah/happy-birthday-louis-pasteur/Content?oid=3904810

[13] https://pearls.com/pages/how-pearls-are-formed

Made in the USA
Columbia, SC
11 May 2020